AF574157

HILL WALKING

By the Same Author

CANOE SKILLS AND CANOE EXPEDITION TECHNIQUES
FOR TEACHERS AND LEADERS
CAMPING AND HILL TREKKING
CAMPING COMPLETE
BEGINNER'S GUIDE TO LIGHTWEIGHT CAMPING
CANOEING

HILL WALKING

Peter Williams

PELHAM BOOKS · LONDON

First published in Great Britain by
Pelham Books Ltd
52 Bedford Square
London WC1B 3EF
1979

ISBN 0 7207 1135 5

Typeset in Great Britain by Saildean
Printed by Hollen Street Press, Slough
and bound by J. M. Dent Limited, Letchworth

CONTENTS

PREFACE

I have written *Hill Walking* so that the reader will have, under one cover, the basic information he or she requires to enjoy walking the hills during summer time in safety.

The book outlines the personal, camping and specialist equipment needed for basic walking expeditions and also covers map and compass technique. It explains how to plan an expedition, notes the hazards that can be encountered when walking in the mountains or on moorland and the techniques to employ to avoid or, if necessary, overcome difficult situations. Mountain safety procedures and information on the weather are also included. For those involved in the instruction of young people the book provides suitable information for basic instructional purposes and stresses the need for interesting progressive training leading to well-prepared purposeful expeditions. *Hill Walking* should therefore be of use to both the backpacker on his lowland treks and also to serious hill walkers. I would, however, stress that this book is written to cover the basic skills and techniques required for walking hill country in temperate climates but the reader should always beware of extremes in weather that can be experienced particularly when in remote exposed terrain. However, I have also included methods of combating such conditions if they cannot be avoided.

I hope that this book will be of particular assistance to those charged with the responsibility of leading, organizing or overseeing youth training projects and that it will also help students and teachers to appreciate the need for very careful preparation when planning walking projects in isolated country. Above all, the book should enable the reader to enjoy the romance and challenge of the hills.

I would like to record my appreciation of the advice given by David G. Lloyd, BSc, Scientific Officer of the Meteorological Office on the chapter on Weather, also for the helpful comments on the part on rope techniques given by Flight Lieutenant Doug Leighton RAF., MLTB Mountain Instructor and former instructor at the Joint Service Mountain Training Centre (Wales). I am also grateful to Air Vice Marshal D.W. Atkinson, QHP, MB, ChB, FFCM, MFOM, DPH, DIH, RAF, for his advice on the medical aspects of heat disorders, frostbite and exposure.

1
Personal and Camping Equipment

Clothing

The functions of good walking clothing are to keep the body comfortable, warm and protect the wearer from the effects of wind, rain and cold. Clothing should be sufficient to keep the body temperature within a range of a few degrees and so ensure the efficient functioning of the body. According to the weather conditions, insulation may need to be varied by putting on or removing one or more layers of clothing. Walking in summer conditions may require the walker to wear only a shirt, breeches and socks. On the other hand, conditions at height can vary considerably and it is important to know the qualities of good protective garments. If you intend to walk in colder conditions you must be suitably prepared with the right protective clothing.

Insulation

The insulation of the body against cold is achieved by trapping still air between the fibres in the clothing's weave and between layers of garments. The windproofing of over-garments prevents penetration by wind which will otherwise remove the heated air trapped between the fibres. Over garments and footwear should be water resistant or, better still, waterproof, particularly so when used in cold/wet climates. The overheating of the body can be prevented by ventilating the clothing at the waist, through apertures at the wrists and neck, and also by having the head, face and hands bare. Clothing may be divided firstly into basic clothing that gives comfort and warmth to the body such as vest, pants, shirt and sweater, and secondly, protective or 'shell' clothing which ensures that the warmth generated by the body and held in the basic clothing worn next or close to the skin is not dissipated by the extremes of wind, rain and cold. Shell clothing must be well made, for driving rain will often penetrate seams or joins in a garment unless these are well proofed. Under such conditions there is no such thing as a waterproof stitch hole as every area of a protective garment will be tested - water will travel around corners, along crevices in the material and, assisted by capillary action, even uphill. A well-made protective garment that has fewer areas of stitching and seams is therefore less likely to allow water to get through. Under adverse conditions the body needs maximum protection to avoid heat loss and, at times, the effects of exposure. Legs, body and head need to be well covered and this can be achieved by wearing warm comfortable basic clothing underneath plus good shell or protective clothing on top. Take note that it is advisable to select brightly coloured protective clothing that could, in an emergency, be seen some distance away.

BASIC CLOTHING

Basic clothing needs to be warm and comfortable. Soft wool or 100 per cent brushed-cotton shirts of the lumber-jack type are snug and attractive. String underclothes offer good insulation to the body as warm air is trapped in its cells close to the skin. They should be worn on high-level walks in the colder days of early spring and late summer. Avoid wearing nylon underclothes and shirts as they do not have the warmth of natural materials such as wool and cotton. A fleecy American-type sweat-suit can be worn as an additional garment in cold weather and may be kept on at night if conditions are very chilly. A woollen sweater is a must at height, for even in summer the air temperature on a mountain walk can be quite low. If conditions are very cold two light sweaters will trap more warm air close to the body than a single heavier type and give greater warmth. Long, soft-wool socks will protect the feet and legs. If desired, a second pair of short, wool oversocks will give extra protection and warmth to the feet but should only be worn if there is ample room in your boots so that toes are not pinched or rubbed. Derby tweed, wool or whipcord walking breeches (Fig. 6) are ideal to wear and these are usually fitted at the knee with either buckles or Velcro tabs to give adjustment. Terylene and wool trousers are also suitable for summer conditions as they afford protection to the legs from sunburn and wind, and if wet from a shower they will dry quickly. However, they are not suitable for high-level colder projects. If weather conditions are suitable shorts can be worn but make sure you will not suffer from sunburn or chafing of the skin from the wind.

SHELL OR PROTECTIVE CLOTHING

The Cagoule

A cagoule (Fig. 1) affords maximum protection for the body. The garment is light in weight but gives good cover from head to knees. A high-quality

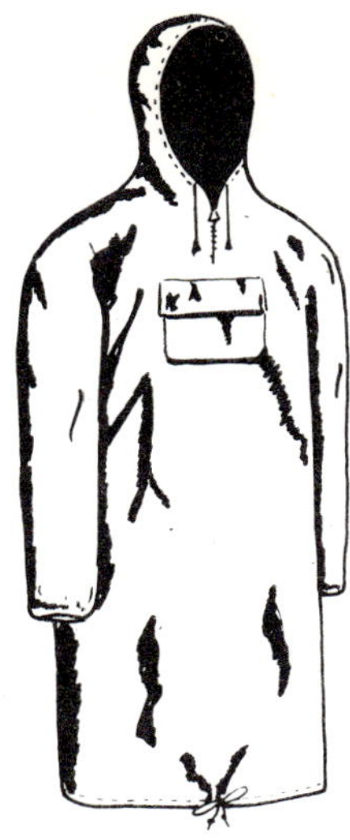

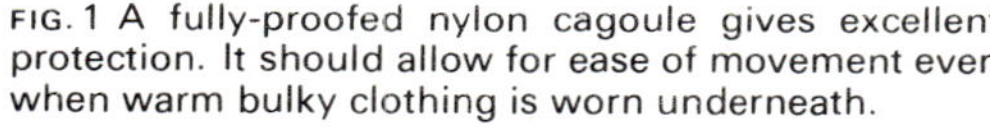

FIG. 1 A fully-proofed nylon cagoule gives excellent protection. It should allow for ease of movement even when warm bulky clothing is worn underneath.

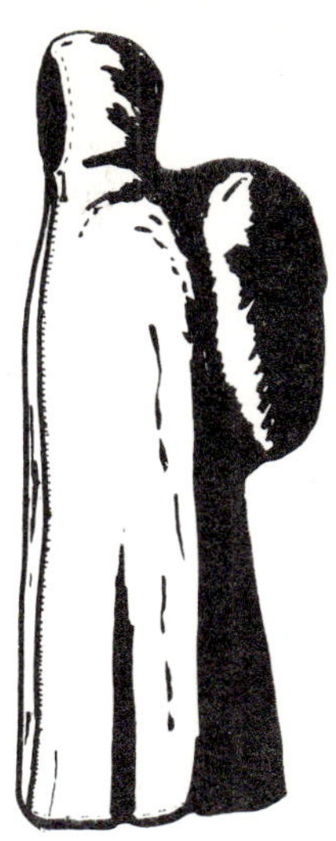

FIG. 2 The Pakjak cagoule-type cape is made of fully proofed nylon and completely envelops the walker and his pack.

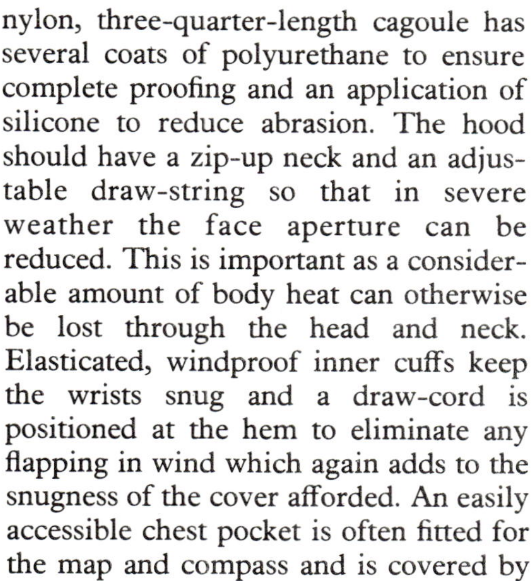

nylon, three-quarter-length cagoule has several coats of polyurethane to ensure complete proofing and an application of silicone to reduce abrasion. The hood should have a zip-up neck and an adjustable draw-string so that in severe weather the face aperture can be reduced. This is important as a considerable amount of body heat can otherwise be lost through the head and neck. Elasticated, windproof inner cuffs keep the wrists snug and a draw-cord is positioned at the hem to eliminate any flapping in wind which again adds to the snugness of the cover afforded. An easily accessible chest pocket is often fitted for the map and compass and is covered by a Velcro- or zip-fastening flap cover. The cagoule can be classed as a survival item for it is possible to sit curled up inside the garment, then bring the knees up and place the feet in a rucksack to obtain maximum protection from the elements (see Fig. 104).

The Pakjak (Fig. 2) is a long, capacious, cagoule-type cape which has no sleeves and completely envelops the walker and his pack. It is made of 11-oz (311 g) polyurethane-coated nylon and is described as a personal mobile storm shelter which is both waterproof and windproof. The Pakjak has draw-cords at the hood and base to make it into a survival bag if necessary and is fitted with a proofed, self-locking, two-way nylon zip which is open ended and runs the length of the front from the neck down.

Fully proofed nylon material does not 'breathe' and can give rise to condensation forming on the inside of the garment. However, recent research with protective nylon clothes has resulted in the manufacture of garments which allow ventilation through minute holes in the material yet still possess their fully waterproof qualities.

Over-trousers

In bad weather, over-trousers (Fig. 3) made of fully proofed heavy-duty nylon give excellent protection to the legs and lower body. In the event of a sudden downpour they should be put on quickly but taken off when the sun breaks through again, to prevent overheating the body. There is therefore no point in having a tight fit as they have to be donned over boots, trousers and maybe a long sweater. A tight fit at the ankle, though stylish, can also give problems unless fitted with a zip. However, take note that a zip can clog with mud or grit and, if fitted, there is no way of shortening trousers that are too long in the leg. Waist fastening is often by elastic but a tie tape is more comfortable. Slit pockets which give access to trouser pockets are desirable but they need to be covered with a flap fitted with press-studs or a Velcro strip to ensure that no water can leak through. When over-trousers are taken off they should be exposed (inside-out) to the air to dry.

FIG. 3 Over-trousers will protect the lower half of the body.

Protective Jackets

The cagoule is a must for the hill walker for, as explained, it is a basic survival item and affords the greatest cover possible for the body. There are several types of jacket that offer protection to the body which are popular with hill walkers. The anorak (see Fig. 4) is a jacket much favoured by youth clubs. It has the same features as the cagoule but extends only to hip length. A draw-cord is located at waist level to ensure snugness. Anoraks are made of nylon with a polyurethane coating to ensure proofing and a silicone finish to resist abrasions.

FIG. 4 An anorak – a useful protective garment, popular with hill walkers.

FIG. 5 The padded Duvet jacket affords maximum warmth. Some designs have a detachable hood.

Other designs are made of closely woven cotton duck, which is hardwearing and windproof but will not normally keep out continuous heavy rain. The Duvet (Fig. 5) is an extremely warm padded jacket favoured by high-level climbers and often made from two layers of waterproof polyurethane-coated nylon with quilted stitching. The filling may comprise polyester fibre or even goose down, which gives great warmth. The front is normally sealed with a heavy-duty all-nylon two-way zip and press-stud fitted flaps protect the zip. There are other miscellaneous jackets in a variety of forms ranging from the smart hunting type to the lighter rambling jacket. The hunting types are made from closely woven fully proofed gaberdine cotton and have an adjustable waist strap, numerous pockets and a concealed hood. Rambling jackets are front opening, have a hood, and are made from coated nylon. Other forms of jacket available resemble the hooded parka design which is padded with polyester fibre to give extra warmth. Many hill walkers prefer a jacket based on the hunting, rambling or parka design. However, it must be appreciated that if open high ground is to be covered in inclement conditions a cagoule and over-trousers should

FIG. 6 Derby tweed, wool or whipcord breeches fitted at the knees with buckles or Velcro tabs are comfortable walking apparel.

always be carried in the rucksack, in case of emergency, for they will provide the additional cover that other clothing cannot give.

GAITERS

Gaiters (Fig. 7) give good protection to the legs and are made of nylon or canvas, or a combination of both. Nylon gaiters are made from 4-oz (113-g) polyurethane-proofed nylon. Most designs have a zip join running up the back of the leg. The gaiter is held in place over the foot by a strong lace which runs under the instep and by a clip that grips the boot lace near the toe. It fits close to the calf and over the boot top. Gaiters are better to wear than leggings for these flap, rub together, get wet and cumbersome and therefore can hinder progress. Gaiters should be worn at any time when the going is wet or muddy – e.g. in long wet grass, damp heather, when crossing marshland or wet peat – even if it is not actually raining.

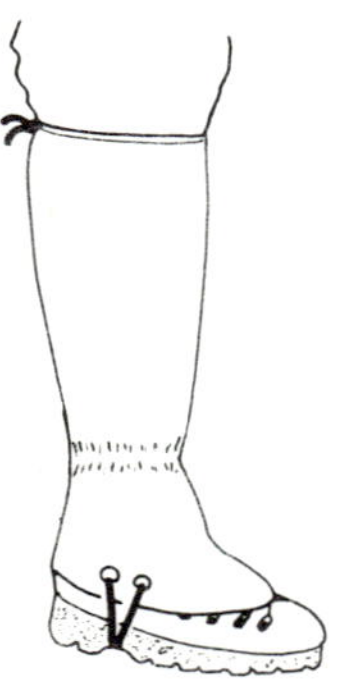

FIG. 7 Knee-length gaiters protect the legs from mud and wet grass. A heavy-duty zip is fitted at the back.

Gaiters do a good job but in doing so they are exposed to much mud, water and grit. At the end of the day they should be dried out and the zips checked to make sure that no dirt is left in the teeth nor in the runner.

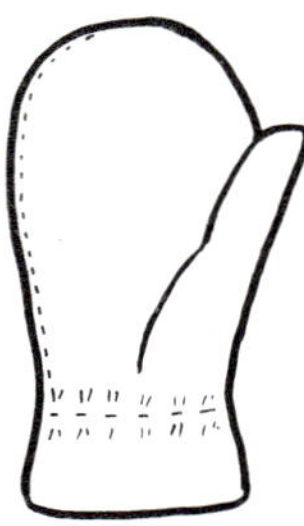

FIG. 8 Wool-lined waterproof mitts for use on high-level walks.

BOOTS

A good pair of walking boots (Fig. 9) are comfortable to wear, give a firm footing in difficult country, protect the feet from extreme conditions of wetness, cold and heat and give support to the ankles.

The construction of the boot is important. A walking boot should be made of soft but strong leather cut from the top section of a hide. The bond between the upper of the boot and the sole needs careful examination for if poorly constructed it may allow water to seep into the boot. Some boots have the upper sewn to the sole and a reinforcing welt rand which runs around the outside of the boot and is sewn to seal the join between the upper and the sole. Other designs have a one-piece rubber sole and heel unit which extends up to also comprise the rand; the upper and sole are bonded together. Another design has the leather upper riveted and stitched to the sole. The walker needs a boot that is more flexible than that of the rock climber, for stiff soles lack comfort and will hurt the ankles. Walking boots should therefore have a slight curve to the sole to permit an effortless heel and toe walking action.

The boot is best made with a soft bellows tongue which is sewn to each side and also to the inside bottom of the lace area to protect the instep and to stop water seeping through the front. 'D' rings and hooks ensure comfortable, firm lacing. A soft, padded ankle and elasticated cuff give protection to the ankle and also ensure a seal at the top of the boot but without causing discomfort or rubbing on the Achilles' tendon.

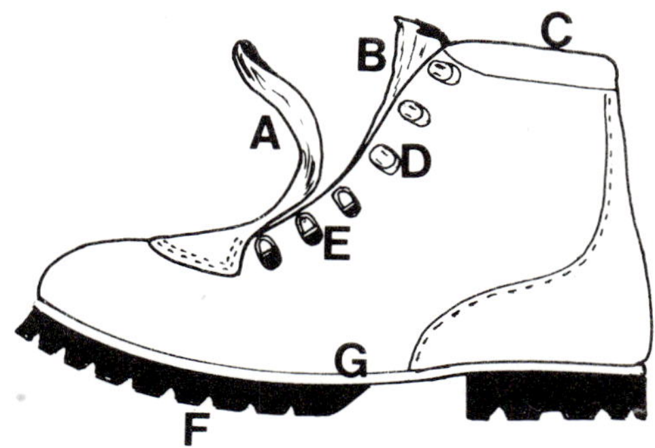

FIG. 9 Features of a good walking boot: A – loose tongue; B – bellows tongue; C – soft padded cuff; D – lacing hooks; E – lacing 'D' rings; F – cleated tread; G – curved, flexible sole.

Some boots have a double cuff. The sole is best made of heavily cleated rubber to give a good grip. Vibram composition soles of non-clog rubber give excellent grip on most surfaces no matter which way the foot pushes. However, care needs to be taken when crossing wet, greasy rock, ice or hard snow, for these surfaces can be treacherous and the tread may not grip.

Boots need to be worn with clean, well-fitting stockings or socks. A single pair of loop-stitched stockings are very comfortable but two pairs of wool socks may be required to keep the feet snug in cold conditions.

No well-used boot will last very long unless it is looked after. Walking in wet grass or heather, or through streams and marshes, will wash out the polish and proofing agents in the leather. After each walking expedition wash off any mud and carefully clean out the grooves in the rubber soles with a stick or knife, also clean the area between the upper and sole. Dry your boots out gradually and never before an open fire. Take note that if some proofing is applied while the boots are damp the agent will be drawn into the leather as it dries out. This action will replenish the oils which were originally fed into the leather during the tanning process and have since been washed away. Once dry, brush off any remaining dirt and then rub in a wax polish to fully proof the leather. Maintained this way your boots should last for years.

Rucksacks and Pack Frames

It is possible to purchase large pack frames and rucksacks that will support a heavy load. However, remember that the motive power for whatever has to be carried is to be provided by you so considerable thought needs to be given as to how you will carry your gear, what you will carry and how it should be packed. Carrying a load across hills requires a pack that is suitable in size and shape and is comfortable to wear. The equipment and personal items to be carried for just a two-day trek with an overnight stop will range from a stove, utensils and food to spare clothing, sleeping bag and tent.

How much should the load be? This will depend on the climate and weather conditions, but the total weight should never exceed one third of your body weight. For young people 30 lb (13.6 kg) is the absolute maximum. There are three types of load-carrying equipment to be considered: the traditional rucksack; the frame rucksack; and the pack frame and sack.

FIG. 10 The Yukon pack – an inexpensive rucksack suitable for day walks or short treks.

RUCKSACKS

The rucksack is basically a container bag that has no supporting frame. It lies directly on the back of the walker supported by two shoulder straps (Figs 10-12). There are many types of rucksack on the market and they are normally cheaper than the frame rucksack or the carrier frame and sack. Some rucksacks are made of 15-oz (425-g) proofed close-weave cotton canvas which is strong and hard wearing but, after heavy rain, it is important to dry out the canvas otherwise it may attract mildew and rot. Nylon sacks are normally made from 7-oz (198-g) nylon that has been treated with a layer of either neoprene or polyurethane so that it will not absorb water. Proofing is normally applied inside the sack so, when loading, take care not to damage the surface with any sharp objects. This type of rucksack may only weigh a little under 2 lb (0.9 kg) but has a capacity of 9-11 gallons (40-50 l).

FIG. 11 A popular design of frameless canvas sack that has a good storage capacity.

Some modern designs are contoured to the shape of the back and the Cyclops range of rucksacks offers a variety of models. Several of these incorporate a removable flexible frame and are constructed from 7-oz (198-g) nylon but the back of the sack, which comes in contact with your shoulders, is made of canvas to give extra durability and help reduce perspiration. Fig. 12 shows the Cyclops-type design. Compared with the framed rucksack or the pack frame and sack, the rucksack is lighter to carry but, unless care is taken when packing, the weight may be distributed unevenly. Having no frame it can serve as a mattress to lie on at night and so stop the cold striking up from the ground.

FIG. 12 The 'Cyclops' rucksacks are contoured to the shape of the back. Several models incorporate a flexible removable frame, others have side pockets and a reinforced suede base.

When considering purchasing a rucksack take note that there should be room for considerable adjustments to the shoulder straps to allow for the wearing of bulky clothing in bad weather. The straps should be about 2 ins (50 mm) in width to take the weight without cutting into the shoulders. Good-sized external side pockets are useful, particularly if they are lined on the inside with additional proofing such as oil cloth. The stove and fuel can then be carried separately with no possible risk of contamination of food or personal clothes contained within the main bag. A pull-out plastic sleeve at the top of the sack fitted with a draw-cord makes for security and ensures the protection of the contents in wet weather. This plastic sleeve can, in an emergency bivouac situation, be pulled out to help protect the body from the effects of cold (see Fig. 104). A large lid flap with long straps will ensure that the tent, which is a comparatively heavy item, can be carried in a waterproof cover on top of the pack and under the flap. The tent will be held securely but being positioned high on the back makes for comfortable walking.

FRAME RUCKSACKS

Modern frame rucksacks comprise a steel or aluminium frame onto which a sack is built (Figs 13 and 14). The frame rucksack distributes the load well and allows adequate ventilation of the back, which is not possible with the frameless type of sack; it also gives a comfortable fit and prevents objects in the sack from digging into the back. Some types of frame rucksack are fairly

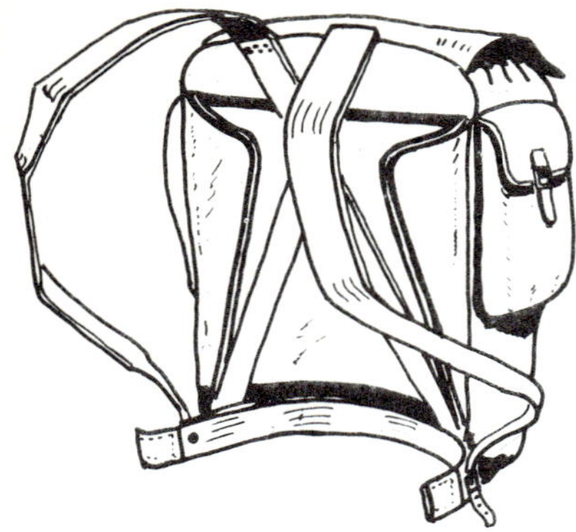

FIG. 13 The Norwegian-type frame rucksack has a crescent-shaped waist support and an aluminium or steel frame onto which the canvas pack is built. Wide, adjustable leather or webbing straps take the load.

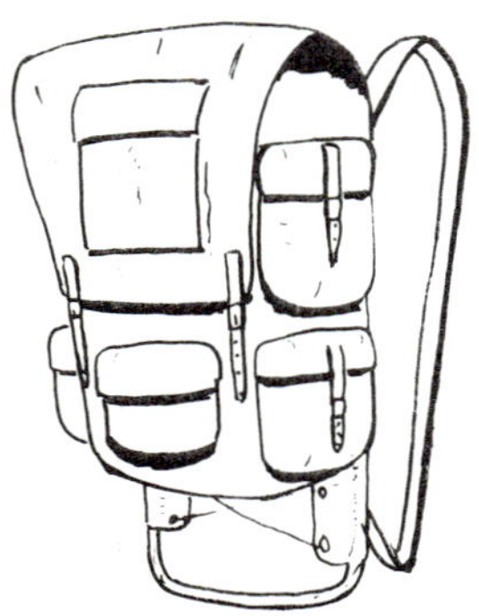

FIG. 14 A high-carry frame rucksack with adequate space below the sack to strap additional light gear, such as a sleeping bag.

narrow at the bottom but widen out at the top being contoured to fit close to the back. They curve over the shoulders to take the body's shape. However, take note that the 'Commando' style of rucksack which hangs low down the back and forces the wearer to lean forward to compensate for the weight is not recommended for walking hills and mountains. Look for a frame rucksack that is comfortable to wear, can be carried high on the back when loaded and has the capacity to carry all the equipment required for your hill expeditions.

PACK FRAMES

The pack frame (Figs 15 and 16) is the most effective way of carrying large or heavy loads. Most frames weigh only

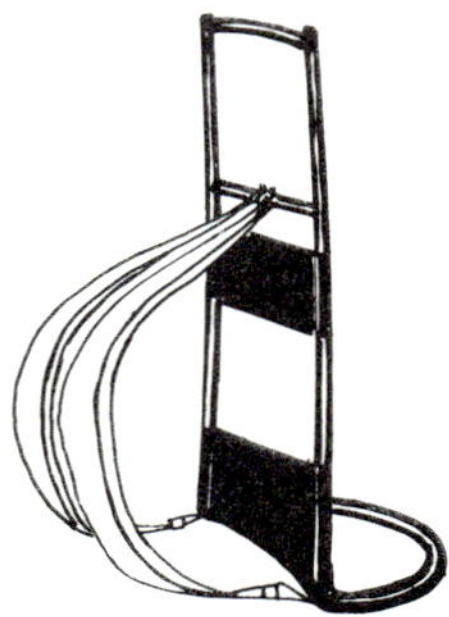

FIG. 15 A light alloy pack frame with strong, well-padded straps. Any suitable purpose-built sack can be attached to the frame.

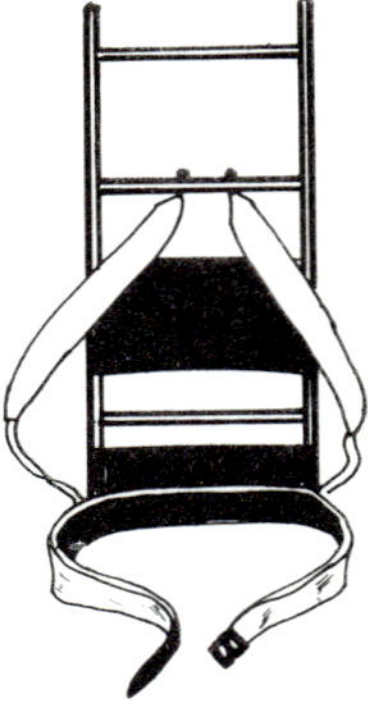

FIG. 16 A padded waist belt helps take the load off the shoulders and gives support. The belt has a quick-release buckle.

$1\frac{1}{2}$-2 lb (0.6-0.9 kg) and are welded together or linked by plastic joints. Some types are adjustable for it is important that the frame fits the walker. Measure vertically from the hip bone to the highest prominent neckbone. The measurement of the pack frame from the top harness attachment point to the bottom of the crossband should equal the distance between these points (Fig. 17). When the pack frame is slipped onto the shoulders it should lie with the top harness point (from which the broad, well-padded shoulder straps run) a little lower than the prominent bone at the base of the neck. The crossband will then sit on the hips. The frame should contour the body and, if used, the padded waist belt with its quick-release buckle should fit snugly around the hips. The padded waist belt will help take the load off the shoulders and give extra support. The correct frame size is particularly important when a waist belt is used for if the frame is too large the movement of the hips will cause the frame to swing from side to side as you walk.

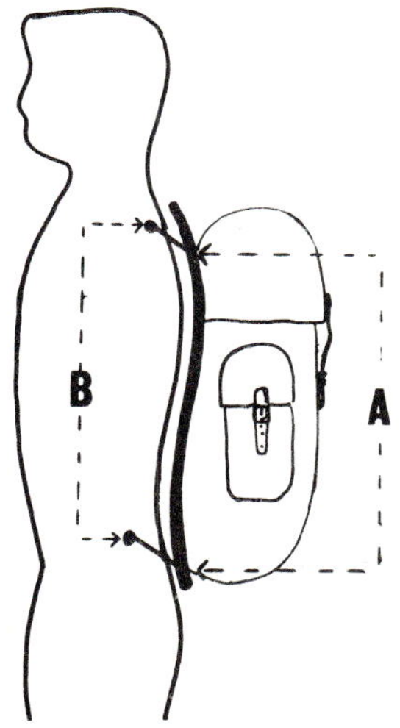

FIG. 17 A pack frame must fit the walker. The measurement between the point of the attachment of the harness and the lower crossband (A) should equal the distance between the hip bone and the highest prominent neckbone (B).

Custom-made sacks can be attached to the frame but it is possible to carry any reasonable form of load from the large service-type kit-bag to a self-designed canvas sack, provided, of course, it is well packed and then strapped securely to the frame. When buying a sack look for the type that has strongly stitched seams to take a good load and big external pockets. If zips are fitted, the large-tooth variety are best as they are less likely to seize up; also, they should be overlapped with generous covers to keep out dust and dirt. Long lid straps and strong buckles will allow for adjustments of the lid according to the size of the load carried inside the pack.

The weight of a nylon sack may range from as little as 1 lb (0.4 kg) to about 3 lb (1.3 kg).

PACKING THE LOAD

Whatever type of carrier used, whether it is a rucksack, frame rucksack or pack frame and sack, the principles of packing are the same:

(a) Heavier items are packed at the top

of the sack as it is easier to carry their weight high on the back.

(b) Emergency items, such as the cagoule, must be readily available.

(c) Last-wanted items other than those in (a) go at the bottom of the sack.

(d) No hard or sharp items are packed so that they press against the back.

A rucksack or pack frame and sack can be packed as follows. The sleeping bag can be carried externally enclosed in a waterproof cover and firmly tied to the bottom of the carrier frame below the sack or placed in the bottom of the rucksack. Other items go into the sack, spare clothes first as they are comparatively light in weight. Any tins of food, together with eating and cooking utensils, are packed higher as they are heavier items. The stove and fuel can occupy external pockets where they cannot come into contact with food and clothing. Food for the day can be carried in one easily accessible pocket or at the top of the sack. The tent, which is the heaviest item, can lie across the top of the sack in its waterproof cover, held firmly in place by the lid and the tightened lid straps. If possible, split the weight of the tent between two people, one carrying the actual canvas and the other carrying the flysheet, poles and pegs. Emergency items that may be needed in the event of sudden bad weather, such as a cagoule, sweater, woollen hat, emergency rations and also first-aid kit and torch, are best packed near the top of the sack in an easily accessible position. Whatever form of carrier is used you may decide to have a day side and a night side. Food, neatly packaged, eating utensils and extra day clothes are packed on one side, with spare clothes placed at the bottom of the sack. The sleeping bag makes up the other half of the sack together with toilet gear, towel and torch. It is good practice to keep spare clothing and the sleeping bag in polythene bags to ensure maximum protection in the event of bad weather, for driving rain will penetrate the smallest gap or flaw in canvas. Of course, if the sleeping bag is carried externally it *must* be protected by a proper waterproof cover.

Whichever way you decide to pack your rucksack keep to the basic principle of heavier items packed at the top. Once satisfied that all items are conveniently and neatly stored in the sack, take note of their actual position and always pack them in the same order. In this way your equipment is easy to find – even in the dark.

When the pack is carried the load should be well balanced and located high on the back so that you can stride out in comfort; so before setting off, check the position of the load and, if necessary, adjust the shoulder straps.

Lightweight Tents

A tent's purpose is to provide cover for the night, keep out rain and retain warmth. The hill walker requires a tent that is both light in weight, yet will withstand strong winds. It should normally have sufficient room for two people to sleep in and, if weather conditions are bad, have adequate space in which to cook. The lightest shelter for the night can be a plastic or nylon bivvy bag or polythene tube tent but these are best suited to low-level camping and are not for serious mountain projects. The choice of tent needs careful consideration. Such factors as price, possible usage each year, weight, experience of user(s) and types of projects envisaged should influence the selection of such equipment. The 'best' type of tent is indeed a very controversial subject with hill walkers and campers, and people often favour designs with which they are familiar. The lightweight ridge tent is still made in large numbers and excellent examples are on the market. Larger ridge tents of 60-160 lb (27-72 kg) are also available and are ideal for use at static base or training camps. However, to appreciate the basic design of any tent it is preferable to understand the functions of the parts of a tent. The design of the traditional ridge tent, which is still very popular and often forms the basis of other design patterns, is analysed below.

TENT PARTS

The small ridge tent (Fig. 18) has two tent poles, normally made up of three sections of aluminium or wood. Aluminium poles are best as wood poles swell if wet and can jam. The ridge is formed by the tautness of the tent canvas due to the pull exerted by the front and rear guy-

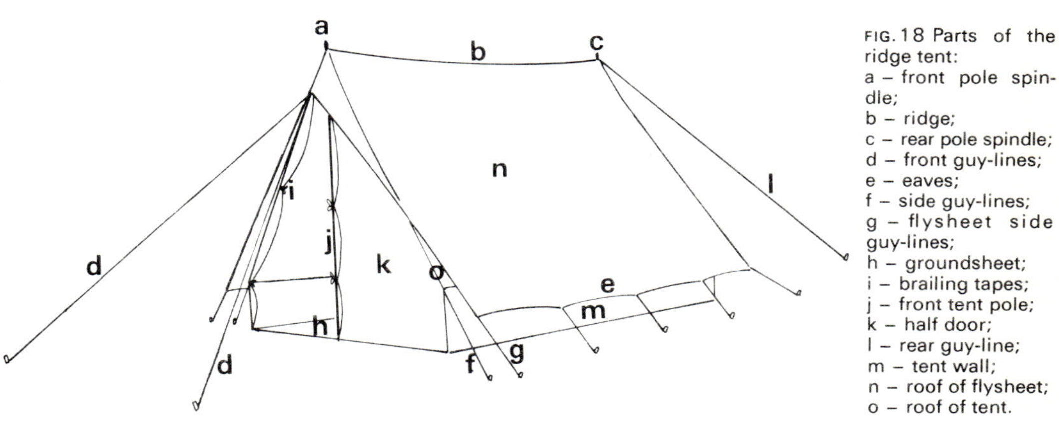

FIG. 18 Parts of the ridge tent:
a – front pole spindle;
b – ridge;
c – rear pole spindle;
d – front guy-lines;
e – eaves;
f – side guy-lines;
g – flysheet side guy-lines;
h – groundsheet;
i – brailing tapes;
j – front tent pole;
k – half door;
l – rear guy-line;
m – tent wall;
n – roof of flysheet;
o – roof of tent.

lines. The ridge canvas is strengthened on the inside by a tape sewn to the roof. Some tents have an adjustable three-sectional horizontal ridge pole of aluminium to hold the poles firmly apart and so tighten the canvas between the poles and ensure maximum height inside. The spindles of the two vertical tent poles are the spikes on the tent poles. If a ridge pole is fitted the spindles will run through a hole in the ridge pole located at each end and so support the horizontal pole. The spindles initially protrude through the peak of the front and rear roof canvas via a grommet, which is a reinforced circular hole.

Guy-lines are lines made of hemp, nylon, or Terylene which are attached to the roof or walls of the tent at the seams and run to metal (Fig. 19), plastic or wood pegs driven into the ground. They ensure that the tent stands symmetrically to allow maximum space inside and they also hold it down under windy conditions. Hemp guy-lines shrink when wet and so have a tendency to pull the tent fabric and open the weave, thus reducing the water-resistant properties and straining the material. Terylene and nylon guy-lines do not shrink and their slightly elastic properties lessen any direct pull on the tent canvas. Guy-lines are often brightly coloured so that tripping over them can be avoided. The ridge tent is supported at each end by main guy-lines strongly sewn to the canvas and which are secured by looping around guy pegs driven into the ground. All guys are adjustable as they run through aluminium or, in the case of larger tents, plywood or dowel slides (Fig. 20) that can be slid up or down the guy-lines to

FIG. 19 Types of lightweight metal tent pegs: a – skewer; b – Atlas; c – Bulldog. The Atlas and Bulldog pegs are particularly suitable for pegging out the main guy-lines as they are stronger and give greater support than the skewer type.

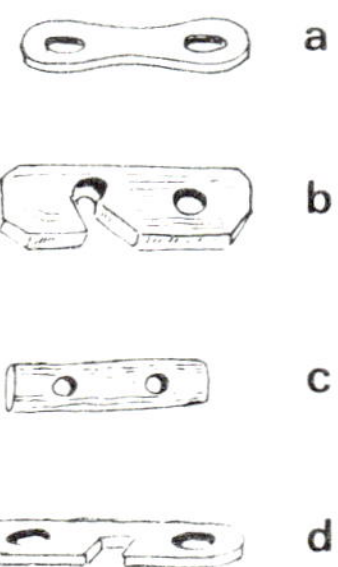

FIG. 20 Types of slides: a and d – aluminium; b – wood; c – dowling.

FIG. 21 When using a metal slide, lock the guy-line into the nick in the slide and it will not slip.

take up or reduce tension on the line and correspondingly on the canvas (Fig. 21). Side guy-lines run out from the tent walls to hold out the eaves and sides of the tent.

In most tent designs, guy-lines are best run out in line with the seams of the tent. The roof of the tent slopes down to the eaves which extend outside the wall and serve to shed rain water away from the tent. The walls of the larger ridge tent are secured to the ground by brailing pegs. Brailing tapes are those tapes sewn to the tent which enable the wall or door to be reefed up in fine weather allowing air to circulate. Wall tapes are normally found only in designs of large ridge tents.

The front of the tent is normally sealed either by a centre vertical zip, a semicircular zip running from the apex of the door down one side and along the bottom, or by tie tapes attached to each half of the door. A groundsheet of rubberized fabric or plastic should form the floor of the tent. It is best sewn into the tent to eliminate draughts coming under the tent walls. There is considerable merit in having a groundsheet that extends 2 ins (50 mm) or so up the side, front and back walls of a tent for in very wet weather no water can then flood the tent.

A flysheet is basically an extra roof that gives additional protection to the tent and camper. A good flysheet will keep the tent waterproof even in very heavy rain for it takes the initial impact of the raindrops and water runs off its sloping surface. In many designs the apex of the flysheet extends forward to form a canopy which affords shelter to the door of the tent. The grommets of the flysheet, like those of the tent, also fit over the spindles of the two tent poles. However, if the flysheet is in direct contact with the roof of the tent, in heavy rain the tent could leak at that point. In some cases a separator - that is, a hollow metal tube about 2-3 ins (50-75 mm) long - is placed on each spindle before the horizontal ridge pole and the flysheet are fitted; this serves to raise the ridge of the flysheet.

The insulation afforded between the tent and the flysheet keeps the tent warmer in winter and cooler in summer. Flysheets that extend to the ground give maximum protection to the tent, for a breeze cannot get under the flysheet to disturb the still air near the walls of the tent. Instead of side guy-lines being used to secure the fabric, rubber suspension bands are often fitted and these hold the flysheet firm but also allow some give in the wind. The flysheet has its own main and side guy-lines.

TENT DESIGN

Recent years have seen considerable variations in lightweight tent design but many tents are developed from basic types (Fig. 22). The number and length of poles used or the shape of canvas can influence their form. Examples are the

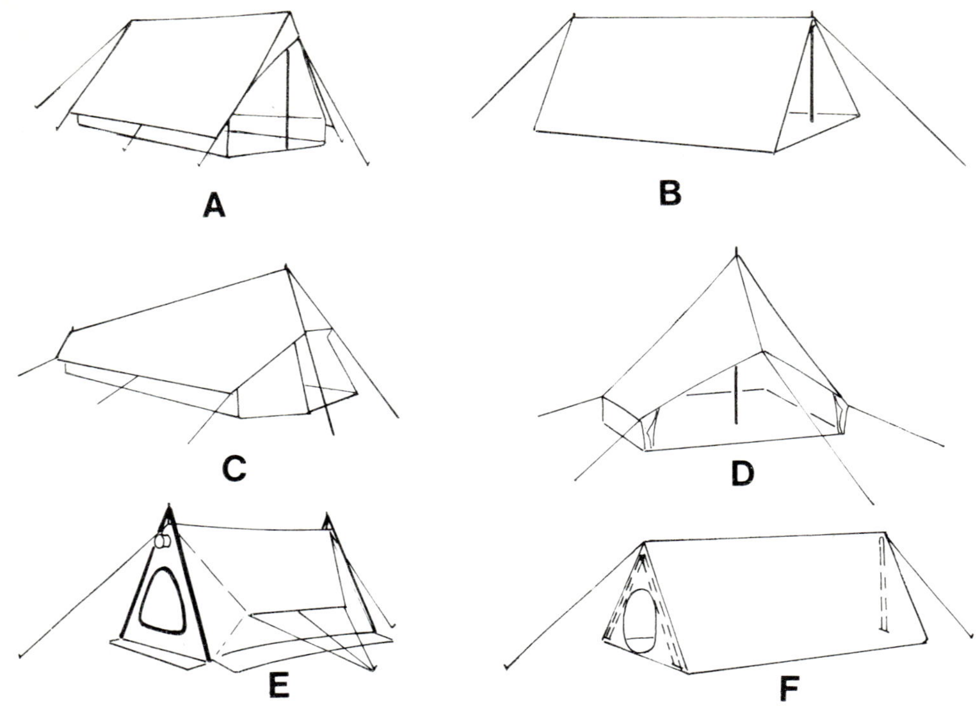

FIG. 22 Some basic tent designs: A – walled ridge tent; B – wall-less ridge tent; C – wedge tent; D – single-pole pyramid tent; E – ridge mountain design with two external 'A' poles; F – internal 'A' pole bivouac tent.

two-pole walled ridge tent (Fig. 22A); the two-pole wall-less ridge tent (Fig. 22B), the wedge tent (Fig. 22C), the single-pole pyramid tent (Fig. 22D), the two external 'A' pole design in which the tent is suspended (Fig. 22E), and the internal 'A' pole bivouac tent which also has a single upright rear pole (Fig. 22F). The design of tents influences their performance in bad weather, the ease with which they can be erected and the internal space available for the occupant(s). The one-pole tent such as the pyramid design can be pitched single-handed, quickly and easily. It is normally lighter than other designs and its front guy(s) take up less ground than the fore and aft guys of the ridge and wedge type. Its shape renders it stable in wind and, being higher, it can be more comfortable to live in during inclement weather. Ridge tents are normally cheaper as they are easier to make. The ridge with no walls weighs and costs less than a walled ridge tent. The steep pitch of the roof sheds the rain well and it will withstand wind better. However, a walled ridge tent is more spacious at floor level and gives more headroom. The use of external 'A' poles ensures that maximum space is available within a tent.

FABRIC AND WEIGHT

In the last few years the introduction and development of synthetic fabrics has made a considerable contribution to tent design. Nylon fabric is now commonly used in the construction of many lightweight tents. However, cotton fabric tents are still a very viable purchase though many enthusiasts prefer nylon tents because of their reduced weight. Ripstop nylon fabric is almost half the weight of cotton loom. It is proofed with a thin polyurethane coating to ensure full weather protection. Nylon will not absorb water like cotton so after a heavy shower most of the moisture can be shaken off the fabric before the tent is packed for the day's trek. However, nylon does not possess the same breathing qualities as cotton and unless adequate ventilation is built into the design of the tent condensation will form on the walls of the inner tent. If silicone-coated walls are used in the design of the inner tent this can allow a transfer of vapour-laden air and condensation is not such a problem. Nylon may be affected by the ultra-violet rays of the sun which causes a breaking down of the fabric structure. However, many modern designs are made of high-tenacity ripstop nylon fabric which has inbuilt ultra-violet inhibitors to prevent the tear strength of the material deteriorating while the tent is in use and exposed to sunlight. On the other hand, cotton loom fabric of about 3 oz (85g) per square yard/metre is a well-proven material. A good cotton fabric tent, fully treated against rain and rot, is an excellent purchase and will last for many years if carefully looked after. Proofed cotton possesses the property of allowing air to filter through the fine weave so that little water from condensation will form inside the tent, yet the fabric is waterproof. Take note that the cotton fibres absorb water when exposed to wet conditions and if the tent has to be carried when wet the all-up weight will have increased considerably. If the tent has to be re-erected in a wet condition in heavy rain the canvas may leak so, if possible, it is always best to dry out the tent before packing it for the next stage of your walk.

The weight of tents that will accom-

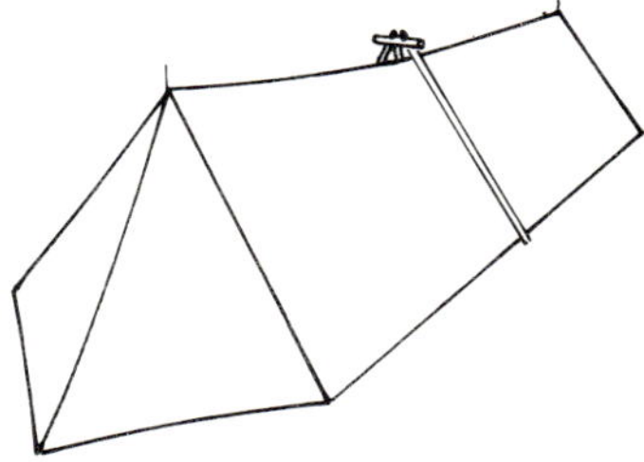

FIG. 23 The Fjällräven Termo G66 is a two-man tent that will withstand extreme conditions. It uses an external 'A' pole and internal poles. Approximate weight: 4 lb (1.8 kg).

modate two people and are suitable for use on hill-walking projects has been cut as low as 4 lb (1.8 kg) including the flysheet. The Fjällräven Termo G66 (Fig. 23) and Marriott Kamplite (Fig. 24) are such examples. Most two-man lightweight nylon designs weigh between $4\frac{1}{2}$-7 lb (2-3 kg) whereas tents more suitable for a lightweight base camp weigh about 8-14 lb (3.6-6.3 kg). Fig. 25 shows the Good Companion Major which, if fitted with external

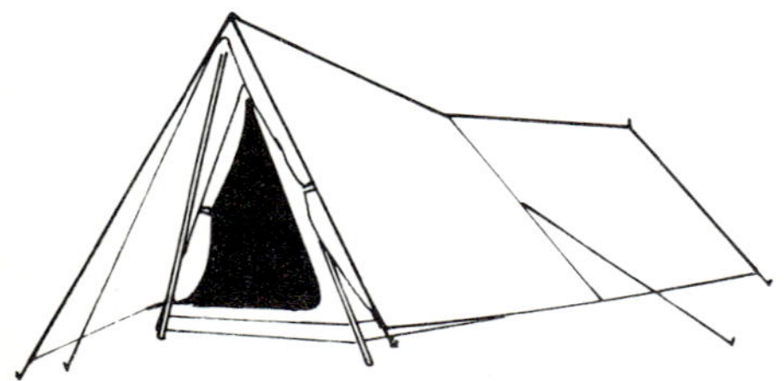

FIG. 24 The Marriott Kamplite sleeps two; is made of nylon and can be erected quickly, flysheet first. Weight: 4 lb 15 oz (2.3 kg).

FIG. 25 The Good Companion Major is ideal for use at base camp. It sleeps up to four and weighs $10\frac{1}{2}$ lb (4.8 kg) if fitted with a single pole or $13\frac{3}{4}$ lb (6.2 kg) with angle poles. Made of high-quality, lightweight cotton.

FIG. 26 The Marathon MKIII is an all-year-round design. Nylon. Sleeps two.

poles, will sleep four; it weighs $13\frac{3}{4}$ lb (6.2 kg). It should be appreciated that many 'mountain' tents are designed for use by climbers operating at altitude in cold dry conditions and are not suitable for the cold, wet conditions which are often experienced in Great Britain.

Sleeping Bags

The purpose of a sleeping bag is to keep you warm by insulating the body from cold air and also from any dampness striking up through the ground. The degree of insulation afforded is dependent on the type and amount of filling and its arrangement within the sleeping-bag walls. A sleeping bag is used for about six to eight hours each night and, in bad weather or winter time, you will spend an even longer period enjoying the warmth and comfort it can offer. After a long day's trek adequate comfort and rest is necessary to refresh both body and mind. The sleeping bag is therefore a very important item of kit; when it comes to choice there is really only one – the best you can afford.

FILLINGS

Modern sleeping bags contain natural fillings such as down and feathers or man-made fillings such as plastic foam, Tricel, Terylene and Dacron. Down is the underplumage of geese and ducks. Nothing that man can manufacture has the qualities of loft, softness, compressibility and lasting resilience possessed by this natural substance. A down bag can be very light yet will keep you very warm. Light down, which comprises very fine fluffy feathers, gives the best results. Heavier feathers do not have the same thermal properties. The quality of fillings can be assessed by three main criteria - filling power, softness and durability. Filling power is measured as the volume occupied by a given weight of uncompressed filling. With down it depends on the size of individual down clusters and partly on the condition of the down. Filling power may, for comparison purposes, be related to a given weight of filling so that one ounce of uncompressed down will perhaps fill twice the air space taken up by one ounce of a different filling. Softness is a subjective assessment that is easily made for you can soon tell the advantages of down over feather fillings or the considerable difference in the feel of down and kapok fillings. Down and feather are durable fillings. A good down sleeping bag that is used occasionally should last a life-time and, even if well used, should last many years. It should be appreciated that any filling which is 'reclaimed' tends to be brittle and break down into small pieces that have limited filling power so it is important to know the quality of the filling. The British Standards Institution (BSI) lays down specifications: 'down' bags must be at least 85 per cent by weight down, the remaining filling must be composed of small fluffy feathers; 'down and feather' bags must be at least 51 per cent by weight down; 'feather and down' must be at least 15 per cent by weight down. Take note that a filling described as 'down' or 'feather' may be partly or wholly reclaimed. However, under BSI regulations a bag described as 'new down' must comprise 100 per cent new filling. Down, therefore, is the best type of filling for it has little bulk, little weight but high efficiency and is suitable for use on mountain walking projects. A mixture of feather and down from waterfowl or soft curled feathers are also good natural warm fillings. Down has few failings but it will not work well if damp and, if really wet, will not keep you warm at all so it is most important to protect your sleeping bag from the elements.

Cotton-wool sleeping bags are not a good purchase as the filling is easily crushed. The thickness of the walls is then reduced and so are the thermal properties of the bag. Kapok-filled bags are also of limited value for kapok has a tendency to lump and lose its original even layer.

The last few years have seen the

growing popularity of excellent synthetic fillings such as Tricel, Dacron and Terylene. Tricel is a low-priced filling that provides the warmth necessary for low-level summer camping. It is light, soft, resilient and crimped to give the warmth required. Dacron is a polyester filling which is light, warm, non-allergic and odourless. A well-made Terylene-filled bag of about 4 lb (1.8 kg) can be used all the year round though is not suitable for use in very cold conditions.

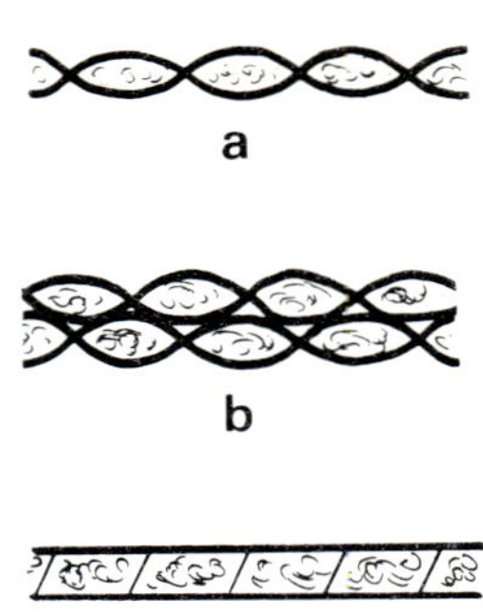

FIG. 27 Cross-sections of sleeping-bag walls: a – inner and outer covers drawn together by quilting stitches, forming cold spots; b – two layers of simple quilting will eliminate cold spots and provide excellent insulation; c – box-wall sleeping bags have fabric dividing walls that retain the filling and ensure a constant thickness without cold spots.

CONSTRUCTION OF SLEEPING BAGS

The problem faced by manufacturers is that of producing a bag that has a uniform thickness of filling right around the body. The filling has to be restrained so that it does not move or slip within the walls. This is done by dividing the walls into squares, sections or tubes. Some bags are made in a manner where the outer wall comes in contact with the inner wall along the line of quilting stitches (Fig. 27a). The area of the lines of stitches form cold spots because of the lack of thickness and insulation at these points. This type of quilting is unsuitable for colder conditions or where bivouacking techniques are to be employed on a high-level lightweight trek unless you are prepared to wear additional clothing when you go to bed, such as woollen tights, track suit, a wool shirt and socks.

However, where two layers of simple quilting are used in the construction of a sleeping bag the insulation is excellent and cold spots are eliminated (Fig. 27b). This arrangement is employed in the type of bag that is virtually two sleeping bags, one inside the other. Boxed or walled sleeping bags are more expensive than the single-walled quilted bag but a better purchase, for the inner and outer walls are completely separate from one another (Figure 27c). The filling is contained in areas or boxes by fabric walls that are stitched to the inner and outer walls. These boxes allow for the expansion of the filling when it is warmed by the body and ensure that there is always a complete layer of filling to insulate the sleeper. A sleeping bag fitted with a draw-cord effect is best, for a bag will only afford maximum warmth if it can seal in the body's heat and the

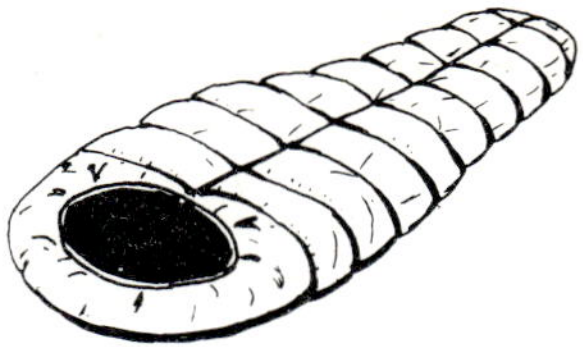

FIG. 28 A sub-zero sleeping bag. The warm duck-down filling is contained in boxed quilting or a double layer of simple quilting.

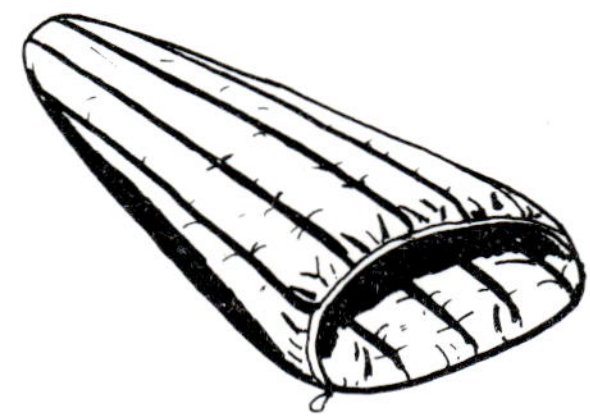

FIG. 29 A double-quilted, Dacron-filled, cold-weather sleeping bag fitted with a draw-cord at the neck.

draw-cord effects this seal. When the cord is pulled, your body from the shoulders down is as snug as the quality of the bag can make you. Some bags are fitted with zips for convenience of entry and exit. Expensive sub-zero bags are often mummy-shaped and designed so that the bag will cover the neck and head. Such designs (Fig. 28) have a draw-string that, in very cold conditions, will close the bag to leave only a small space for breathing. Other designs are shown in Figs 29, 30 and 31.

The coverings of sleeping bags vary: cotton fabric is often used to cover summer designs; cambric and wet-resistant cambric are used for cold weather and sub-zero designs respectively; ripstop nylon is also used to cover some models. A nylon inner lining

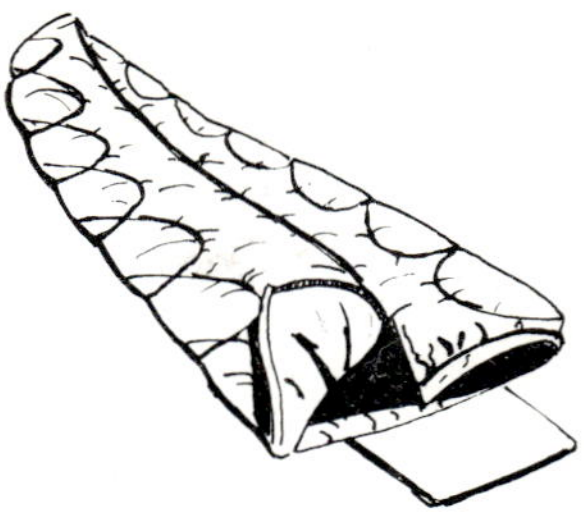

FIG. 30 A lighter design fitted with a short centre zip. The bag can be carried rolled up in its fabric hood which, if filled with clothing, can also serve as a pillow.

FIG. 31 A general-purpose sleeping bag with a short side zip and fabric hood.

provides a smooth finish and permits the occupant to turn easily even though he is enveloped in an inner sheet inside the bag. Wool or brushed-cotton inners are the warmest and other types are made of polyester and cotton or nylon. It is advisable, in the interests of hygiene, to use such a lining sheet otherwise body moisture will be absorbed by the filling of the bag and the inner walls will become dirty.

It is possible to purchase a sleeping bag cover which weighs just under 3 lb (1.3 kg) made with a strong waterproof base and a polyurethane-proofed nylon top. This cover will give extra protection to the sleeping bag and occupant if shelter is limited, as in a bivouac situation.

CARE OF SLEEPING BAGS

The thicker the layer of feathers or down in a sleeping bag the warmer it will be, for heat generated by the body will be trapped among the feathers or down so that the volume of filling lofts or expands. However, under weight, such as imposed by the body, the air is squeezed out of the bag walls and the filling is compressed. It is important that the bag is aired regularly to allow any compressed areas to expand. If the weather is a bit hostile or if you are short of time, a good shake of the bag or a quick whirl over your head once or twice will help air the bag and allow the filling to expand. If conditions are good and time permits, air the bag by laying it over the roof of the tent or over a bush; also, turn it inside out to air thoroughly. A sleeping bag should not be compressed for long as the filling will take time to loft so, if possible, avoid keeping the bag rolled up for long periods and store the bag by hanging it up. Should your sleeping bag become damp or wet, dry it as soon as possible for a damp sleeping bag cannot conserve body warmth efficiently as the down will not loft to trap the air. If the outer cover becomes marked, clean it with a damp sponge but do not use detergents.

KEEPING WARM

In cold conditions the conduction of the body's heat through the earth is the main problem and when the thermometer reads zero you need about 4 ins (100 mm) of down around you to prevent a rapid loss of body heat. To help avoid this loss of heat spread a bed of soft, dry ferns and leaves on the spot where you will pitch the tent. A layer or two of newspaper and a frameless rucksack spread under you will also serve to stop the cold striking up through the groundsheet. A hip-length air bed or foam mat will help keep you warm as well as give extra comfort but, of course, they are fairly bulky items to carry and add an extra weight of about 2-3 lb (0.9-1.3 kg) to the load.

If conditions are quite cold dress up to go to bed and put on thick socks, a woollen track or sweat suit plus a woollen cap. Use all the resources you have to keep warm. Have a hot drink when you retire. A stone that has been heated over the camp fire then wrapped in a piece of cloth and placed in the sleeping bag is a good bed warmer. If you are warm, you will sleep well and rest both body and mind, to wake refreshed ready for the day's trek.

Stoves

There are various types of lightweight stove on the market including those fuelled by solid fuel, methylated spirit, paraffin, petrol or gas. However, several factors need to be considered before purchasing a stove and these involve weight, size, price, and availability and cost of fuel. Information on the boiling time and the one-charge burning time will also give an indication of a stove's overall efficiency.

SOLID-FUEL STOVES

The most popular type of solid-fuel stove is the design that, when folded, resembles a small, flat, light-steel box which measures a little larger than a pack of cards and encloses the solid-fuel blocks (Fig. 32). When erected the stove comprises a pot stand with supporting legs and a burner plate on which the fuel blocks are placed. The fuel blocks will light even when damp and partially used blocks can be put out and retained for use later. Heat control is effected by adding or reducing the amount of fuel on the burner plate. The best cooking results are obtained if lightweight aluminium cooking utensils are used as the stove cannot generate pressure like a paraffin, gas or petrol stove. The solid-fuel stove has no working parts that can malfunction. The Hexamine type is a well-proven British Service issue that is also available on the open market. Another similar make is the Esbit stove made in West Germany. The solid-fuel Tommy stove (Fig. 33) is another varia-

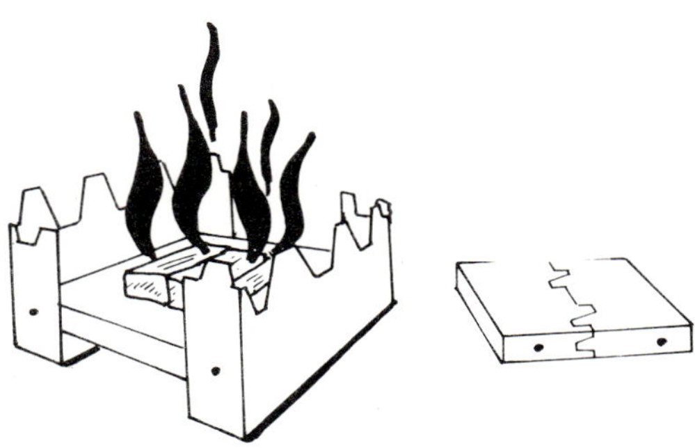

FIG. 32 A solid-fuel stove. The hinged feet can be adjusted so that small cooking utensils may rest on the pot stand. When folded (*right*) it will act as a container for the fuel tablets.

FIG. 33 The Tommy solid-fuel cooker.

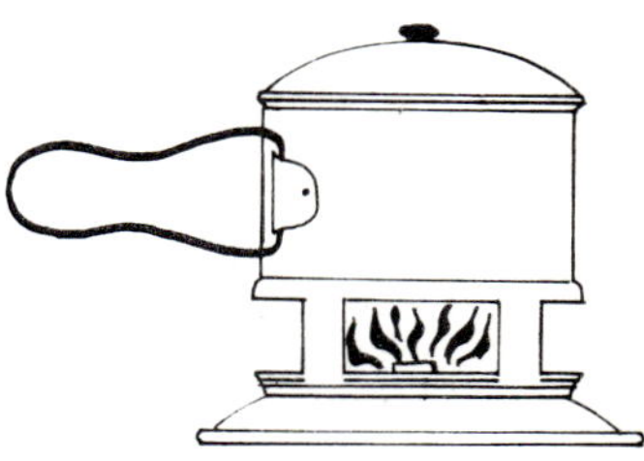

FIG. 34 The Meta boiling set comprises a self-contained saucepan, solid-fuel burner and stand. Capacity: $\frac{1}{2}$ pint (0.2 l).

tion of this form of stove but one in which the fuel is ignited within a round metal stand. The Meta boiling set (Fig. 34) is a light aluminium kit that weighs 3¼ oz (92 g) and includes a saucepan of just over ½ pint (0.2 l) capacity and a cooking stand. It is specially suited for heating small quantities of liquid.

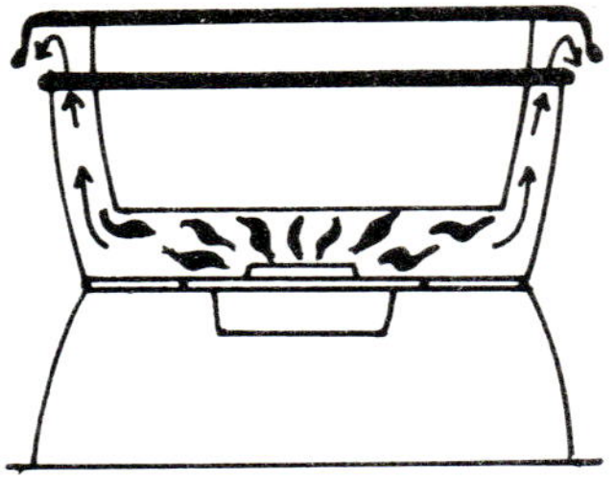

FIG. 36 A cut-away drawing showing how the meths-burning Trangia Storm Cooker 25 works. This stove will boil 1¾ pints (1 litre) of water in about 8 minutes.

METHYLATED-FUEL STOVES

The methylated-fuel picnic stove is the cheapest and one of the simplest types of lightweight stove available. Like the solid-fuel stove it is extremely reliable. The Express-type (Fig. 35) weighs 8 oz (225 g) and measures 4½ ins (115 mm) in diameter by 3 ins (75 mm) high. The stove has no working parts but comprises a hollow steel cup with a perforated rim. This stands inside the combined pot stand and wind shield. Meths is poured into the cup to a level indicated and then a match applied to the centre of the cup ensures a flickering flame that soon settles down to form a very effective gas-like ring of fire that emits from the perforated rim. The disadvantage with the methylated-fuel picnic stove is that it is not possible to control the heat output and it uses a fair amount of fuel. A 2-oz (56-g) charge of fuel will burn for 29 minutes in calm conditions at 72° F (22° C); long enough to heat several dishes; the stove will boil ½ pint (0.2 l) of water in 5 minutes. Take note that it is most important to check that the flame is completely extinguished before more fuel is poured into the cup otherwise the meths could flare up and cause a serious accident. However, sensibly used, this simple cooking device is safe and 100 per cent reliable. The Trangia Storm Cooker 25 (Fig. 36) is a more advanced design of meths stove and comprises an aluminium cook set with two large frying pans, frypan and pot lifter. The stove will boil 1¾ pints (1 lt) of water in 8 minutes. The Storm Cooker measures 4¼ x 9 ins (110 x 230 mm) and weighs 2½ lb (1.1 kg).

FIG. 35 A cut-away drawing of a methylated-spirit picnic stove that is an inexpensive but effective cooker. The fuel container is housed within a combined wind shield and pot stand.

PARAFFIN PRESSURE STOVES

The Primus type of paraffin pressure stove (Fig. 37) is a Swedish invention well known throughout the world. It is cheap to run and will give a long burning time. The stove has a high heat output but it is also possible to control the pressure from a very low to quite intense heat. The paraffin pressure stove works on the principle of vaporizing paraffin by compressing air. The burner of the stove is first heated by a priming of meths or solid fuel set on fire in a cup specially designed for this purpose and located midway up the stem of the stove. A few pumps are then given to the main reservoir and a match applied to the burner enables the paraffin vapour to catch. The stove will then commence to roar so that the spreader ring glows red hot. The Primus 96L (½ pint/0.2 l), Hipolito (1 pint/0.5 l) and Blaxburner (2 pints/1.1 lt) are popular paraffin pressure stoves of this type. I have used a ½ pint (0.2 l) Primus for many years and found it a very reliable stove that is not affected by dampness, rain or intense cold. However, you cannot afford to neglect a pressure stove. The jet requires to be cleaned from time to time and after much use the pressure washer may need to be renewed. The Primus 96L model is ideal for lightweight projects. It has a ½ pint (0.2 l) fuel reservoir and weighs 28 oz (0.8 kg) empty. It will boil 1 pint (0.5 l) of water in just over 5 minutes. One charge of fuel, which weighs 7 oz (198 g), will last for approximately 140 minutes. The Optimus 111 paraffin stove is a more recent design housed in a folding steel box. It has a capacity of 1 pint (0.5 l) of fuel and will burn for about 2 hours on one filling. The stove weighs 4½ lbs (2 kg).

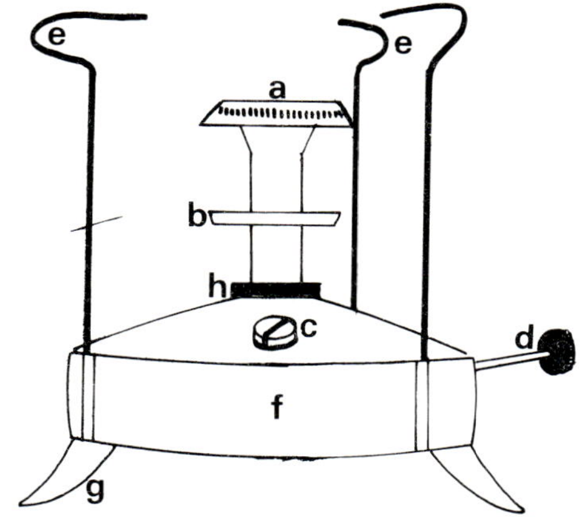

FIG. 37 A ½-pint (0.2-l) paraffin pressure stove: a – flame spreader plate; b – ignition cup; c – fuel cap; d – pressure pump; e – detachable pot stand; f – fuel tank; g – folding legs; h – screw thread for central stem.

PETROL PRESSURE STOVES

Petrol stoves (Fig. 38) are not recommended for use by the inexperienced or young as the fuel is highly volatile. It should be noted that stoves sold in Great Britain are normally intended for use with unleaded petrol. There are various excellent petrol-fuelled pressure stoves on the market such as the 1-pint (0.5 l)

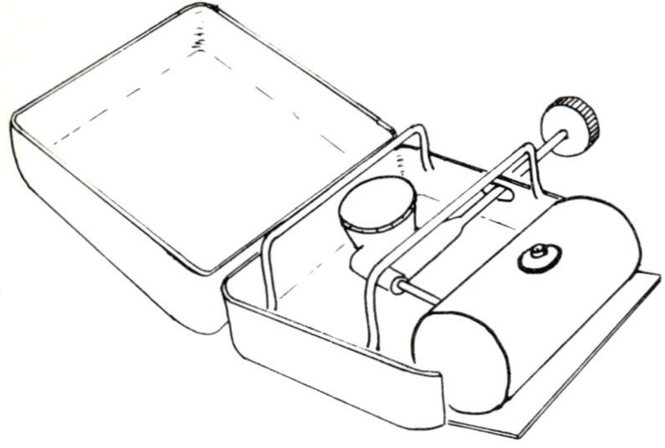

FIG. 38 A ½-pint (0.2-l) petrol stove in its case with pot stand erected. It has a regulating burner and safety valve.

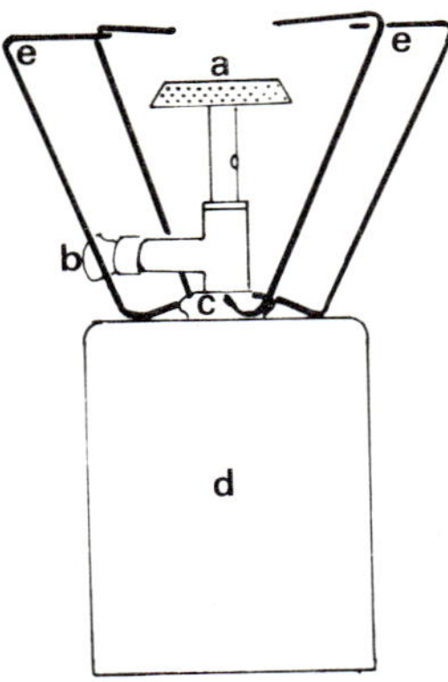

FIG. 39 A lightweight gas stove. The parts are: a – gas ring; b – on/off valve; c – screw thread union with cartridge; d – disposable gas cartridge; e – pot stand.

capacity Optimus 111B which weighs just over 4 lb (1.8 kg) or the smaller ⅓ pint (0.1 l) capacity Optimus 8R which weighs only 1½ lb (0.6 kg). It will burn for about 45 minutes on a single filling of fuel that weighs 3 oz (85 g). Petrol gives off toxic fumes when burnt so care needs to be taken if the stove is used inside a tent. It is extremely important that the manufacturer's instructions are read carefully so that you know exactly how to use and service your petrol stove.

LIGHTWEIGHT GAS STOVES

Generally speaking lightweight gas stoves (Fig. 39) are not expensive to buy but cost more to run than liquid-fuelled paraffin or petrol stoves. The advantage of gas is that it is clean, requires no priming and the pressure can be finely controlled. There are numerous designs of lightweight gas stoves on the market made by such firms as Camping Gaz, Veritas, Tilley and Falk. Generally speaking, a gas cartridge with a capacity of 6-8 oz (0.1-0.2 kg) of gas will give over 2 hours of burning time. However unlike other types of lightweight stove, as the fuel commences to run out the pressure will drop considerably for quite some time and delay cooking. Take note that when butane gas is used at low temperatures difficulty can be experienced in lighting the stove and the stove may then burn with little pressure. Propane gas however will burn well in cold conditions.

Utensils

At the absolute minimum only two vessels are needed for cooking on an expedition, a frying pan and a pot. There are numerous good lightweight canteens on the market (Fig. 40) that comprise both

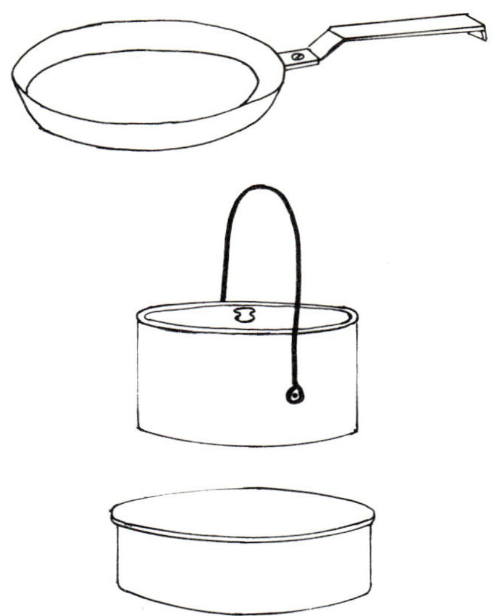

FIG. 40 A good lightweight canteen will comprise a minimum of frypan, boiling pot and cooking dish. When packed, the items should fit neatly one inside the other.

cooking and eating utensils. When purchasing such equipment make sure that the items are also compact - a rucksack has little spare room for bulky gear - so look for the type which has utensils that will fit neatly inside one another. A two-man canteen need not add up to more than 1½ lb (0.6 kg) in weight. Cooking pots should be seamless to avoid possible leaks and a wide base makes for quicker cooking and less fuel used. When considering lightweight frying pans check for stability when on the stove, particularly those types which have long folding handles. If the weight of the handle outweighs that of the light pan and its contents it will be unstable and could be dangerous unless the handle is continuously held throughout the whole cooking operation. Utensils that incorporate the paint-pot type of handle are not designed for the handle to stay upright away from the heat. You will therefore need a grip handle that weighs only 1½ oz (40 g) with which it is possible to handle these and any other hot utensils with safety. The examples overleaf illustrate some of the types of canteen on the market and their size and weight.

It may be necessary to purchase items separately and excellent cheap light aluminium saucepans and frypans are sold by Messrs Woolworth. British Service-type mess tins are very durable but as they are made of thick-gauge aluminium they are therefore fairly heavy and are not suitable for use with stoves that have a limited heat output. A polythene mug is light and almost unbreakable. A 1-pint (0.5-l) enamel mug is a handy size and can be placed near a camp fire to keep the contents warm. An aluminium mug will absorb the heat from the liquid and can burn your lips even when the contents are quite drinkable. For eating, at the minimum you need one deep soup plate, mess tin, or dish. This can be washed between courses and will provide a vessel for soup, stew and even more complex meals. The clip-together lightweight knife, fork and spoon set is a good purchase and there are a number of designs on the market. Don't bother to carry the cumbersome kitchen type of tin opener; the 'Baby' type, well known

Canteen Set:	*Hiker* (1 person)	*Gilwell* (2 persons)	*Wanderer* (1 or 2 persons)	*Two-man* (2 persons)
Comprises:	2 x 7 in. (177 mm) frypans and detachable handle 1 x 5 in. (127 mm) saucepan, lid and detachable handle 1 x ½ pint (0.2 l) mug	1 x 2 pint (1.1 l) saucepan 1 x frypan 1 x plate/lid	1 x 7 in. (177 mm) frypan 1 x 6¾ in. (171 mm) dish 1 x 6 in. (152 mm) plate 1 x 2½ in. (63 mm) deep boiling pot with lid	1 x 7 in. (177 mm) saucepan 1 x 7 in. (177 mm) frypan 1 x 6 in. (152 mm) frypan 2 x 6 in. (152 mm) plates 2 x mugs detachable handles
Weight:	12 oz (340 g)	16 oz (453 g)	15½ oz (439 g)	18 oz (510 g)

to Service men from their 'compo' ration packs, is strong, light and simple to use.

When on a mountain trek water supplies would normally be obtained direct from fresh springs. However, if a lightweight base camp is to be established and there is space to carry such items as collapsible water carriers, these can be very useful. A 1-gallon (4.5-l) capacity collapsible polythene bottle or

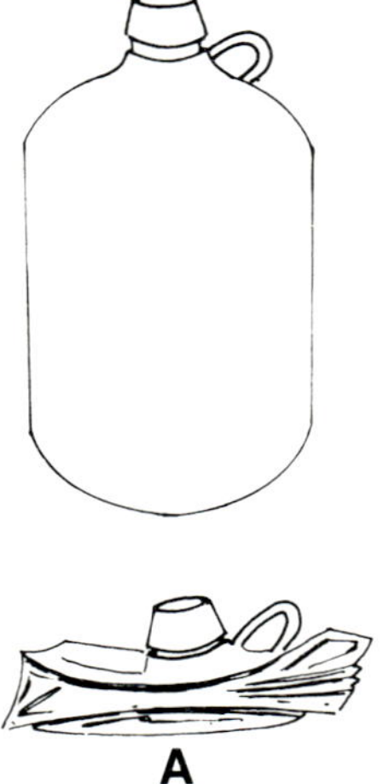

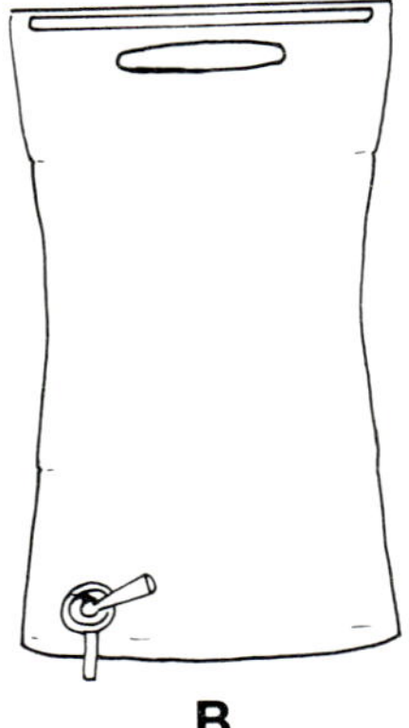

FIG. 41 If a base camp is to be set up collapsible 1-gallon (4.5-l) capacity polythene bottles (A), or roll-up polythene water carriers fitted with a tap (B), are very useful.

an equally light roll-up polythene water carrier fitted with a tap are suitable designs (Fig. 41).

It must be stressed that when on a trek the weight of items carried must be kept to a minimum. However, light polythene jars of 8½-fl oz (250-ml) capacity are useful for carrying dry rations such as sugar, tea, coffee, etc. If fresh eggs are to be carried one or two eggs, well packed, may fit inside the canteen or mess tin or, if space permits, it is possible to obtain a light plastic egg box with a hinged snap lid that will take six eggs.

Remember, when selecting equipment it is normally advisable to buy the best you can afford.

2
Camping Techniques

The object of this chapter is to outline the basic techniques for setting up camp and for ensuring comfort and safety.

It is advisable to look for a suitable camp-site at least two hours before sunset. This will give you time to find a good pitch then set up camp and make supper before darkness falls. Even though you are on a moor or in the hills you are on someone else's property. If it is possible, such as when there is a farm nearby, you should always ask permission to camp. When trekking more remote country the site selected may be miles from anyone. Nevertheless you have an obligation to ensure that you do not spoil or damage the area in any way and it is extremely important that the Country Code is adhered to at all times (see Appendix A). When selecting a camp-site look for an area that offers protection from the prevailing wind, such as a hollow in the ground, or one that has a natural windbreak such as a sheepwall, trees or clumps of bushes. When on an open moor even a fold in the ground or a slight bank can offer some protection. However, it is often impossible to select a site that is completely ideal. Some points to observe when seeking a site in hill country are as follows:

(a) Select a sheltered, well-drained, level area. The site should be free of stones and grass tussocks. Short, springy grass indicates dry ground.

(b) Take note that clay soil is brick-hard when dry, gluey when wet and always drains badly; therefore a tent pitched on clay soil in wet weather can give problems. On the other hand, gravel and sandy soil drain well.

(c) A tent pitched on a slope can make for an uncomfortable night's sleep. If you have to use a sloping pitch, sleep with your head up the slope.

(d) A site near a clear stream has considerable advantages for there is water for drinking, also for personal washing and washing up dishes. The cool water can also be utilized to keep food supplies fresh (see page 46).

(e) Do not camp in a gully if the weather is suspect. Evidence of debris such as driftwood may indicate that in the event of a flash flood, even some distance away, the gully will become a watercourse.

Low-level sites have additional peculiarities that should be noted:

(a) Thick, lush grass usually indicates ground that holds water. Long grass will retain the dew and, even after a shower, remain damp for a long time. If one particular patch of grass is much greener than the rest it normally indicates that the ground is very damp and therefore not suitable as a pitch. It may also be liable to flood in heavy rain.

(b) Fields that are abundant with nettles and thistles are best avoided as they usually harbour flies and gnats.

(c) Don't pitch your tent under trees; the branches will drip long after a shower and keep the canvas wet. In high winds branches can break off. The base of a tall tree is also a hazardous place to be during an electrical storm.

(d) If there is evidence of mosquitoes and gnats select a spot exposed to a fair breeze, for these insects rarely fly in such conditions.

Figure 42 shows the features and layout of a developed lightweight base camp.

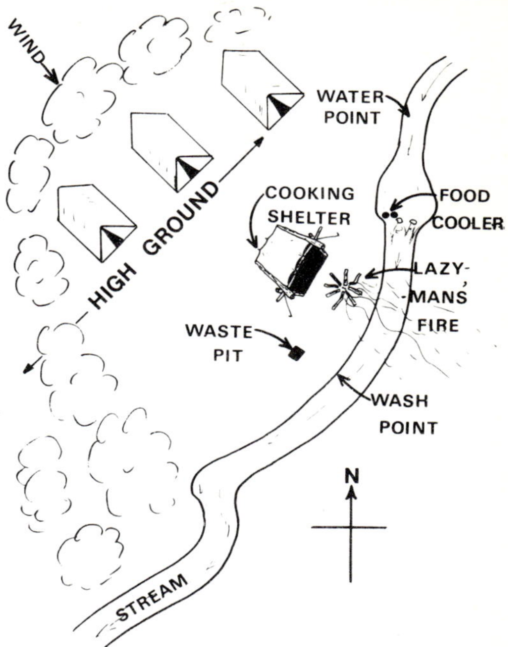

FIG. 42 A developed lightweight base camp in a sheltered area; note the economical layout.

Making Camp

Setting up camp requires a number of tasks to be undertaken:

(a) Tents to be erected.

(b) Kit to be unpacked, sleeping bags unrolled and beds made.

(c) Perishable foods protected by placing in a cool place.

(d) Water obtained and purified either by boiling or using purifying tablets.

(e) If the camp is to be a standing base camp then waste and latrine pits will need to be dug and perhaps firewood collected for a camp fire that can also be used to dry wet clothes.

TENT PITCHING

It is important that each member of the party is familiar with his equipment and can erect, strike and pack his tent with speed. This ensures that in inclement conditions there is no delay in securing cover from the tent and, in really hostile weather, can lessen the possibility of exposure.

The following methods of erecting a two-pole ridge tent, a single-pole tent and an angle-pole 'A' tent refer to those types of tent which have a sewn-in groundsheet.

(a) Two-Pole Ridge Tent

(1) Select your site and note that your tent should back into the prevailing wind. If the weather forecast is very good and you wish the tent to face east or south-east to have the sun in the morning, check the direction that the door must face.

(2) Note how the tent is folded to fit into the canvas bag, and the arrangement of and folds in the flysheet.

(3) Spread the tent on the ground and untie the guys.

(4) Insert the pegs through the metal or plastic rings set in the base of the tent and the groundsheet, starting at one corner of the tent, going to the next to ensure that the groundsheet is fully extended and not puckered.

(5) Put in the front and back main guy pegs at nearly a tent's length away. Hook the guy-lines on and adjust so that they are slightly slack (Fig. 43A).

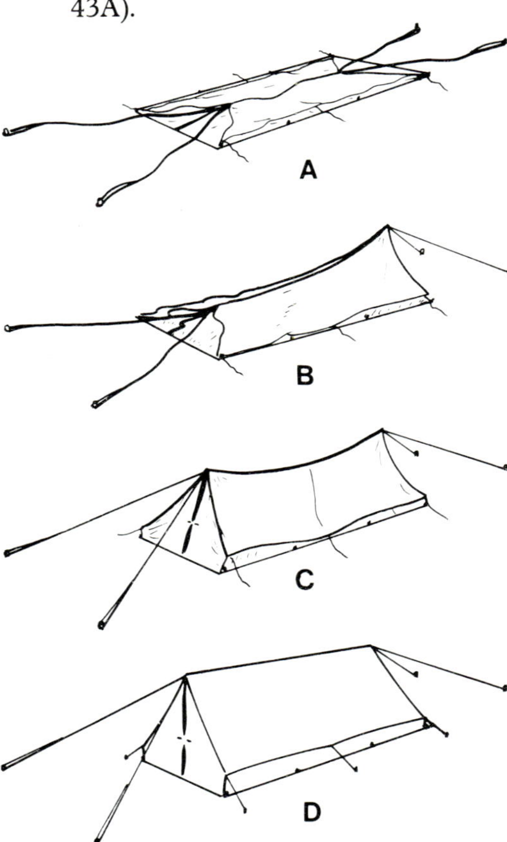

FIG. 43 Stages of erecting the two-pole ridge tent: A – the groundsheet is pegged, then the main guy-lines are run out and pegged; B – the rear pole is inserted; C – the front pole is inserted and the door secured; D – side guy-lines are pegged out, then all guy-lines tightened.

(6) Erect the poles and insert the rear spindle into the ridge hole (Fig. 43B).
(7) Insert the front pole spindle into its ridge hole then lace up the front door (Fig. 43C).
(8) Run out and peg the wall guys.
(9) Finally, adjust all the guy-lines so that the ridge is straight and the tent has no unnecessary folds. The side guys should normally be in line with the seams, following the same slope of the roof, and the pegs should be at an angle of 45° to the ground. The poles should stand vertically. The walls of the tent are thus fully extended and the canvas is symmetrical (Fig. 43D).

(b) Single-Pole Tent
(1) Spread the tent on the ground and untie the guys checking that the door is facing the correct direction. Also take note of the points outlined in paragraph (2) above.
(2) Insert the pegs through the metal or plastic rings set in the base of the tent and the groundsheet, starting at one corner of the tent, going to the next to ensure that the groundsheet is fully extended and not puckered.
(3) Put in the front main guy peg at nearly a tent's length away (Fig. 44A). Hook the guy-line on and adjust so that it is slightly slack.
(4) Erect and insert the tent pole and lift upright (Fig. 44B); secure the door then adjust the main front guy. Now peg out the wall guys.
(5) Finally, adjust all the guy-lines so that the tent has no unnecessary folds. The side guys should normally be in line with the seams, following the same slope of the roof, and the pegs should be at an angle of 45° to the ground. The pole should stand vertically. The walls of the tent are thus fully extended and the canvas is symmetrical (Fig. 44C).

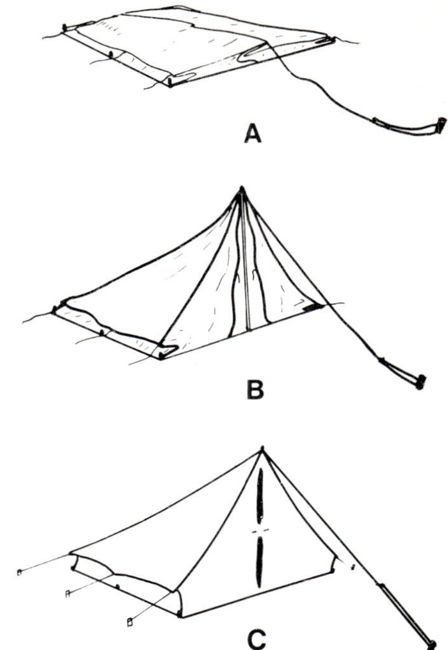

FIG. 44 Stages of erecting a single-pole tent: A – the groundsheet is pegged, then the main guy-line is run out and pegged; B – the pole is inserted, the door has yet to be secured; C – side guy-lines are pegged out then all guy-lines are tightened.

(c) Angle-Pole Tent

The same procedure is adopted for the erection of the single angle-pole tent (where the tent is suspended from a hook fitted under the apex of the external pole) as for the single pole tent except that the pole is external. When you erect an external two-angle-pole ridge tent (where the tent is suspended at the front and rear) the tent is erected in the same sequence as for the two-pole ridge tent. This sequence of events also applies to the erection of that type of 'A' tent where the tent poles are slid into sleeves in the front and rear canvas (Fig. 22F).

Once your tent is up, drape the flysheet over the top and then peg it evenly to the ground making sure that it does not touch the roof of the tent at any point. If it does touch, rain may seep through at the point where the canvas meets. Take note that there are now lightweight designs of tent that can be erected with the flysheet put up first and taken down last so that in bad weather the inner tent can always be protected.

COMFORT

It is not possible in a book of this size to cover all aspects of lightweight camping but here are some tips that make for good organization, warmth and comfort at camp:

(a) Cover the area on which the groundsheet of the tent will lie with an even layer of soft, dry bracken, heather, grass or leaves so as to give extra insulation to the tent.

(b) If space permits, carry a small wool blanket to cover the floorspace or the area where you lie.

(c) A layer of newspaper placed beneath the sleeping bag will also help the body to retain its heat.

(d) Pieces of newspaper can be placed under food stocks to protect them, kept under pots and pans to prevent the tent floor becoming dirty, put under wet boots and packed inside them to help dry them out, and also used to help start off a fire. In very cold conditions newspaper can be worn under a sweater to give additional insulation to the body.

(e) Take off wet boots and clothing outside the tent. Store boots outside until they can be dried out. Wet clothing can be kept in polythene bags within the tent.

(f) Use the area under the flysheet that is within easy reach of the tent door as a store for boots, the stove and cooking utensils.

(g) Keep the tent tidy by selecting and maintaining set positions for your equipment, e.g. keep the torch in an easily accessible position at the foot of the sleeping bag near the door; keep your watch, wallet and matches in one of the pockets in the tent inner. Similarly keep your compass and map in a set safe place for ease of reference and also to prevent damage to either.

(h) If the tent has no flysheet take care that neither your equipment nor your body presses against the weave of the tent roof or walls otherwise the tent may leak in wet weather.

(i) Candles used for lighting will provide a degree of heat but make sure that they are safely mounted and that the tent has adequate ventilation. Similarly ensure that any other type of lamp is safely mounted and that ventilation is adequate.

(j) If conditions are cold, warm a clean, dry stone in the camp fire and then wrap it in a towel or piece of rag and place it in your sleeping bag before you retire. It will provide heat and comfort for a long time.

(k) At a base camp rig up a cooking shelter as indicated in Figs 45-49 using a 10 ft (3 m) square of canvas to which tie tapes have been sewn.

(l) If there is adequate timber available at base camp and the site is suitable, a cooking fire will serve to conserve stove fuel, dry out wet clothes and also is a good morale raiser in inclement weather. However, only use driftwood or dead wood and do not damage trees to obtain timber.

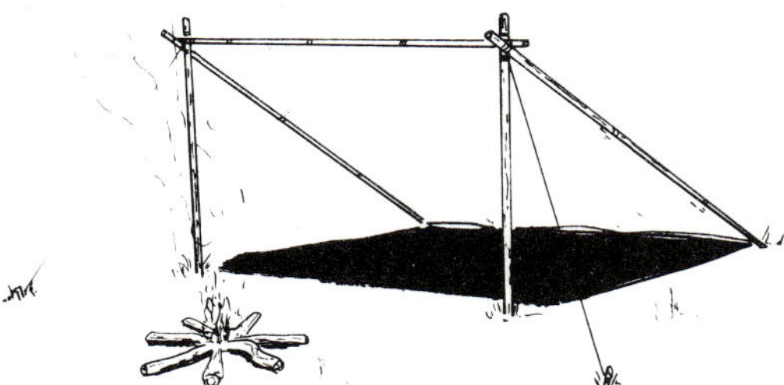

FIG. 45 A lean-to shelter constructed from canvas tied to a frame of sticks lashed together. Also shown is a lazyman's fire which requires little fuel and burns slowly.

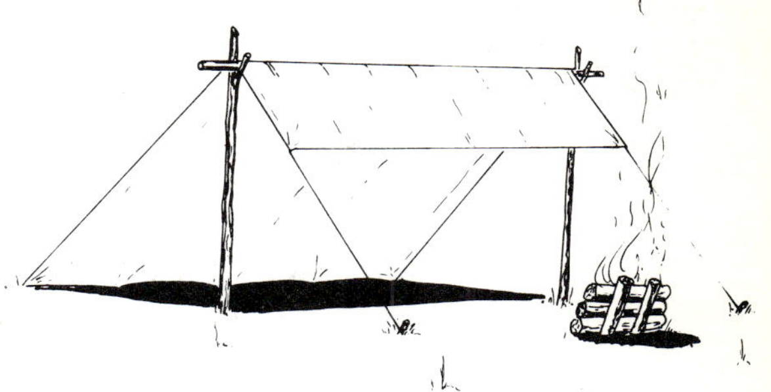

FIG. 46 A lean-to shelter that will give good protection against rain. The reflector fire comprises half a teepee fire (see Fig. 48) built against a wall of logs or a large stone. In this way the fire's heat is reflected into the shelter.

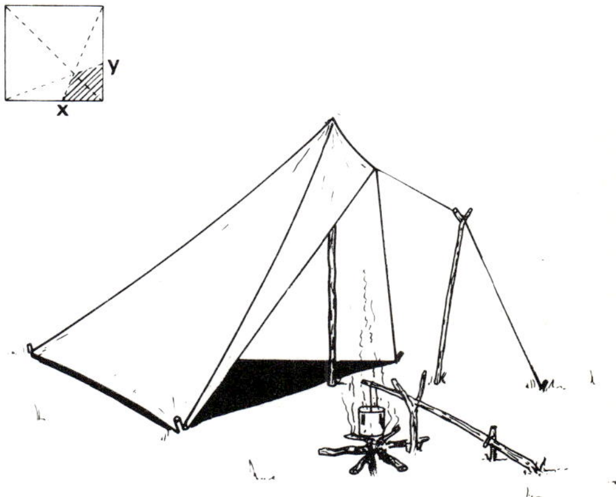

FIG. 47 An American forester-type shelter that can also serve as a good bivouac. To construct the peak of the shelter fold under and tie together the tapes at X and Y. The fire shown is the slow-burning lazyman's fire that will keep the contents of a can simmering while supported on a gin pole

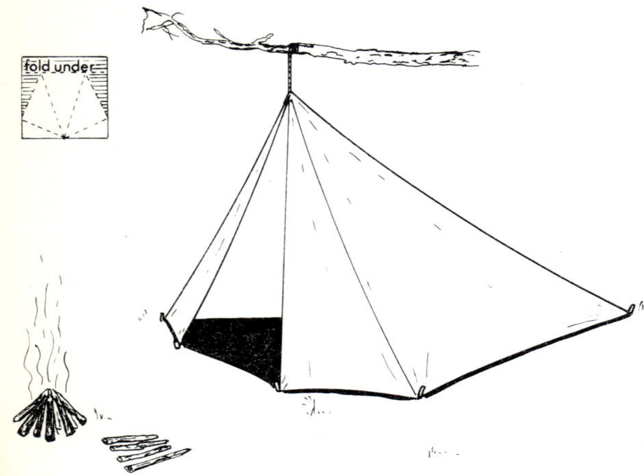

FIG. 48 A half pyramid shelter that can also be used as a bivouac. To form the shape of the canvas fold under the back flap and the two adjoining triangles. The teepee fire will burn well but needs a fair amount of fuel.

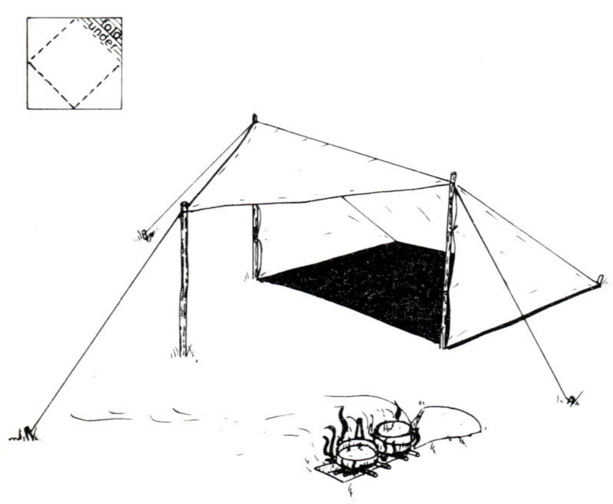

FIG. 49 The American backwoodsman's Baker tent makes a good shelter or bivouac. To form the shape of the canvas fold under one corner. The trench fire is laid in the ground with the end of the trench fanned out to catch the prevailing wind.

BAD WEATHER

Even if the weather conditions seem fine make provision for bad weather when pitching the tent, for the weather can change very rapidly in the mountains. A tent pitched on a still evening to face into the morning sunshine without consideration of the prevailing wind can give a very uncomfortable night if conditions change and the tent is then caught in a high cross-wind. If there is doubt about the weather, weight down the valance of the tent with stones. Stones can also be placed on pegs to ensure that if the wind should rise they are not dislodged by the pull of the canvas on the guy-lines (Fig. 50). Each tent should be a self-contained unit with its own stove, fuel, water, food and utensils so if prolonged bad weather occurs the best possible comfort and protection is afforded the occupants and they will not have to venture out until the rain subsides or the dense wet clouds clear. Fig. 51 shows how a ridge tent can be storm rigged.

Hygiene

WATER SUPPLIES

Generally speaking, mountain springs and streams above the level of human habitation are usually safe to drink. However, if you are uncertain of the

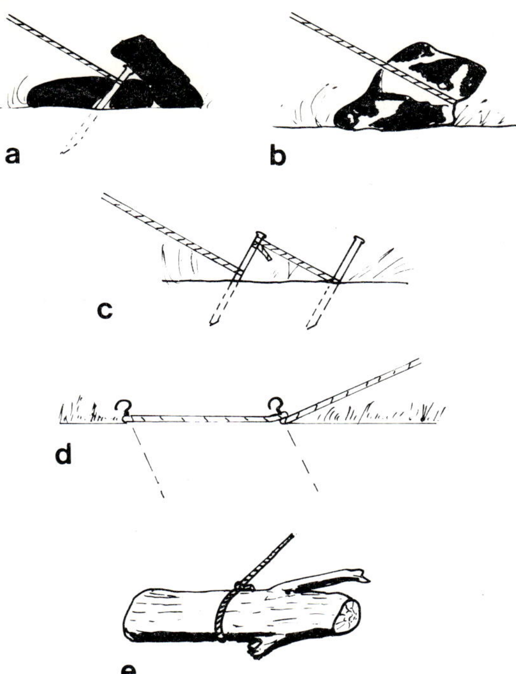

FIG. 50 Securing guy-lines in bad weather: a and b – using rocks; c and d – double pegging; e – tying onto a heavy log.

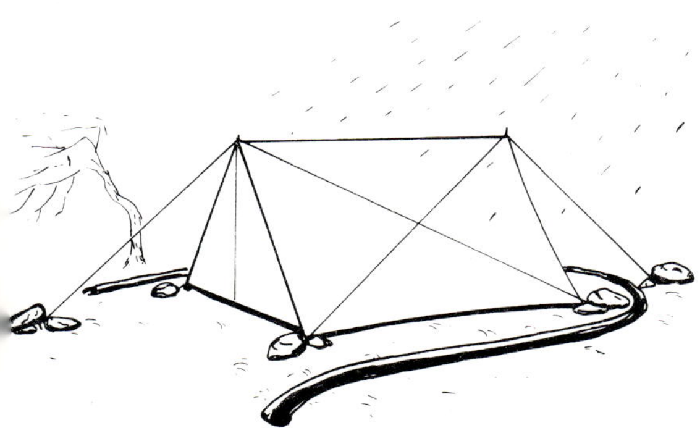

FIG. 51 Ridge tent storm rigged. Rocks secure the guy-line pegs and additional storm guys run from each pole spindle. Note the drainage trench.

quality of your water supply always boil the water or use one of the chemicals designed to make it safe. Water should be boiled for at least three minutes, then left to cool. Pour water from one clean container to another to aerate the water so that it is pleasant to drink. Water can be purified by adding two Helazone tablets to each quart (just over a litre) then leaving it to stand for thirty minutes. If you camp near a clear stream and intend to use the water, avoid stagnant back-waters and take supplies from fast-running parts and always upstream of cattle-watering areas. In the interest of hygiene, do any personal washing downstream of your water point, for the process of washing may also disturb the stream bed.

PERSONAL CLEANLINESS

Next in the order of hygiene priorities comes personal cleanliness. Living in the open should not in any way cause you to slacken your attention to personal hygiene. Wash and clean your teeth regularly and have a good sponge-down each day. However, you need a real soap bath to clean your body properly so use the shallows of a mountain lake or river for this purpose, and perhaps wash out dirty clothes at the same time. Shaving in cold water is no problem provided you have a good blade - it is, in fact, extremely invigorating. Nails should be kept short and clean. Hands must be washed before handling food and after going to the toilet.

FOOD PROTECTION

When at camp food has to be protected from the heat of the day, from dampness in the air and in the ground, also from insects and animals. Food that is exposed to heat or is kept too long can be dangerous to eat. The tent is not a good place to store food when conditions are warm. The coolest places to keep food are in a container in the shade, in the ground or in cold water. Make use of a nearby stream to cool perishable foodstuffs and put butter in a waterproof container, such as a screw-top can or Tupperware jar, then place it in shady shallows with a stone on top to keep it in place. Meat or bacon can be similarly treated and kept in a can or waterproof container in shallows (see Fig. 42). However, unless the container is ventilated, meat will go off, so make holes in the top then cover with muslin to prevent insects from entering. Bottles of milk can also be kept cool if placed in fast shallows with a ring of stones around them, or a cord tied from the neck of each bottle to an overhead branch to stop it being washed away. Cold water and muslin also provide an effective cooling method for milk: stand a bottle of milk in about 1-2 ins (20-25 mm) of water then wet a piece of muslin and drape it over the bottle, the ends being submerged in the water. The water will cool the milk by creeping up the muslin and evaporating.

A hole in the ground lined with stones will make a good, cool larder, but, if possible, select a point in the shade. Food in containers such as polythene bags or Tupperware jars can be placed in the hole and the top covered with green branches and leaves to insulate the cool air in the hole from the warmer air above. Mark the spot to avoid broken or twisted ankles.

Dampness may be present in the air and in the ground, so sugar, biscuits, cereals, and salt should be kept off the ground in airtight containers. Cover all food so as to avoid contamination by insects. If you have a problem with foxes or farm cats and dogs an improvised food bag or safe, hung at a suitable height from a bough, will keep your supplies secure.

CAMP CLEANLINESS

Wash dishes and pots immediately after a meal, for in summer time flies can be attracted by food residue and leftovers. It is best to first wipe the dishes clean with grass to reduce the amount of waste left. The grass can then be burned or buried.

Water from greasy pans will contain particles of food and if tipped on to grass to soak away can, in time, attract rodents and insects and also smell unpleasantly. A grease trap dug in the ground about 1 ft (300 mm) across by 2 ft (600 mm) deep with dry grass laid over twigs on top will filter out and retain food particles and grease. After use, the grass can be removed, burnt and new grass laid.

Keep the inside of the tent clean, neat and tidy. Air your spare clothes and sleeping bag regularly by hanging them exposed to the sun and wind. Turn the sleeping bag inside-out to air thoroughly and allow the filling to expand. Changes in the weather, and particularly muggy weather, will cause condensation to form on the walls of the tent and on the groundsheet so, when conditions permit, leave the door reefed up and, if need be, dry the floor with a rag or newspaper. Sweep out the tent from time to time.

Containers made of glass are not suitable for camping purposes as they can break and anyway they are not necessary - screw-top airtight polythene containers are both lighter and more durable. Plastic bags may also be used in order to keep down weight. If glass jars or bottles are used, take great care that they are not smashed as broken glass could injure livestock. Open tins are similarly dangerous and polythene bags can be lethal if swallowed by animals. If possible, take your rubbish with you until it can be deposited in a dustbin. If this is not possible consumable rubbish should be burned and tins flattened then buried deep in the ground, taking care to replace the turf afterwards.

Toilet arrangements should depend on the length of stay at a site. If a standing camp is to be set up from which groups of people will set out on training walks then adequate toilet arrangements must be made. The most simple arrangement is to erect a hessian or canvas screen to the leeward side of the campsite, supported by stakes, guylines and tent pegs. A crouch-over pit is dug inside the screen about 2 ft (600 mm) deep by about 1 ft (300 mm) wide and about 4-6 ft (1.2-1.8 m) in length. A spade is left near the pit to ensure that a few spadefuls of earth are thrown into the pit after the facility is used. With a larger group at camp it will be necessary to dig separate urinals in the form of a long narrow trench. Less primitive arrangements may comprise the erection of two wooden bars set close together to serve as a seat, and toilet paper located in a tin or enclosed in a polythene bag to keep out dampness. On a standing camp arrange a canvas bowl nearby with a water container, soap and a towel. Encourage people to wash their hands after using the facility. Once the pits are filled with earth and the turf relaid, mark the area with a foul-ground sign - two diagonally crossed sticks that form an X bound to an upright stick which is pushed into the turf. However, if you are on a trekking project out in the wilds take advantage of the natural cover available but always use a light hand trowel to dig a hole and then cover over after use.

Fire Precautions

Each year a considerable number of accidents occur caused by the careless use of candles, cigarettes, stoves or cooking equipment, resulting in burns or scalds. As many of these accidents occur when cooking inside a tent it is best to cook in the open whenever possible. However, in bad weather conditions it will, at times, be impossible to cook outdoors. Cooking in a small tent is not an easy operation for the inexperienced and considerable care should be taken to make sure arrangements are as safe as possible. The following precautions and hints aim to ensure the safe and proper use of cooking equipment and also highlight other fire hazards:

(a) Personnel should be familiar with the correct use of stoves and cooking equipment before an expedition commences; they should also be aware of the dangers of the misuse of such equipment particularly when cooking in a tent.

(b) Care must be taken to ensure that only the correct fuel for a stove is used and that the manufacturer's recommendations are strictly observed.

(c) When a stove is being refilled or a gas cartridge replaced this must be done in the open and away from any naked light.

(d) Do not over-fill a liquid-fuelled stove or lamp.

(e) Premature pumping of a paraffin pressure stove or lamp, before the burner has heated to the required temperature, may cause flooding and the stove or lamp could flare up.

(f) When cooking in a tent adequate ventilation must be available as the stove will produce toxic carbon monoxide gas. It is also advisable to ensure that there is quick access to the open in case of fire.

(g) Make sure that the stove is well supported – a flat stone will serve as a good base. Also check that cooking utensils are stable on the pot stand and will not tip. Handles should be clear of flames and heat. When a pan is stirred support the handle so that it will not tip.

(h) If any adjustments are to be made to a stove, remove cooking pans.

(i) At night and when resting remove gas stoves and cylinders from the tent, for any gas leakage could accumulate in the tent at ground level. If not discovered the gas could rise further to overcome sleepers with fatal results. When gas escapes and collects there is also the high risk of an explosion and immediate fire.

(j) Don't smoke while in your sleeping bag and never sleep with a candle burning.

(k) Don't use long candles, the broad-based slow burners are best. It is important to have a firm base for a candle. A piece of hard, thick card-board about 4 x 4 ins (100 x 100 mm) with a nail or long tack driven through the centre of the card into the base of the candle will ensure that the candle cannot topple.

(l) Take great care when making wood cooking or camping fires. Turf should be removed where the hearth is to be located and the site should be clear of vegetation such as trees, long, dry grass or bushes that could ignite from a spark. When the fire is extinguished, douse the area thoroughly with water and then replace the turf.

FIRE IN A TENT – IMMEDIATE ACTION

(a) In the event of a small fire smother the flames with a sleeping bag but make sure you can get out of the tent if you have to.
(b) In the event of a stove catching fire, throw it out of the tent.
(c) If the tent catches fire, collapse the tent by removing poles and guy-lines.

Striking Camp

A lightweight camp may be little more than a few tents and their contents, a couple of stoves, plus eating and cooking utensils. A training camp may be more developed and include a camp cooking fire, a cooking shelter, a stone- or turf-constructed refuse incinerator, latrine and washplace. However, generally speaking, when you strike camp you work in reverse order to the way you set it up. Non-essential items are dealt with first. Any camp gadgets such as shelters are dismantled and wet and dry pits filled in. Cooking gear and stoves can be cleaned with a Brillo pad. Wood ash on a wet rag is a good natural cleaner and will scour off any blacking and grime. Personal gear should be stowed as it was originally. Wet items should be put in plastic bags to keep them apart from dry clothes.

If a fire has been lit, as on a standing camp, all rubbish should have been consumed by the fire, which was then left to burn itself out. The hearth should be flooded with water so that there can be no possibility of any heat remaining which could cause the fire to flare up when you have gone. Finally, replace the turf where the fire has been located.

TENT STRIKING

Tents that are damp or wet should, if possible, be allowed to dry before packing. This is particularly important if cotton or canvas tents are being used, so an hour or so waiting for the breeze to blow sufficiently or for the sun to rise high enough to dry the canvas can be time well spent. If the tent is really dry you can leave the camp site knowing that you need not look at your tent until the next time it is required, be it the next day or next year. Remember that if a cotton tent is packed wet it will not be completely waterproof until it has dried out, so, should you have to pitch the tent again, rain on the already wet fabric could render it porous. This is where the use of a flysheet has great advantages as it will protect the inner tent fabric from the direct force of the rain, and the inner tent, though perhaps damp, will give adequate protection. However, if a tent is left wet for a few days or more the material will start to lose its water-repellent properties, eventually become mouldy and brittle and could be completely ruined, so it is important to dry it out as soon as possible.

Notes on how to strike the various types of tent are given below. Remember that with some lightweight designs it is possible to fold up the tent under the protection of the flysheet.

Two-pole Ridge, Single or Angle-pole Tents

(a) Ensure that the inside of the tent is clear of all kit and that it is clean and dry. Remove the guy pegs leaving the main guy pegs until last. As you lift out each peg, clean and replace it in the peg bag.

(b) Allow the tent to collapse slowly and remove the tent poles, then roll up and tie the guys, finally the main guys.

(c) Drape the tent canvas to the shape required for packing, then remove the pegs attached to the groundsheet and base of the walls.

(d) Begin to fold the tent and, as the under-surface of the groundsheet is exposed, wipe off any earth and moisture before folding the tent completely. If need be, wait until the underneath is fully dry before the tent is finally packed.

(e) Pack the tent poles into a separate bag if one is provided.

(f) Slip the tent, poles and pegs into the main carrying bag, not forgetting to pull the draw-string and tie so that it is impossible for any part to slip out.

On a standing camp the latrine and washplace are normally the last items to be dismantled then the latrine trench is filled in and the turf replaced. If the washplace has a sump-hole for taking waste water, fill it in and replace the turf. Mark the position of the latrine trench and that of the waste pit with a foul-ground sign as described on page 47. Any new campers to the site can therefore avoid these areas. Make a complete sweep of the area as a final check of its cleanliness before you move on. Also check that no equipment is left behind such as tent pegs or even a piece of string. When you leave, the site should have been returned to its natural beauty, unspoiled and ready for the next walkers to enjoy.

Should you require more detailed information on expedition camping then *Beginners' Guide to Lightweight Camping* (Pelham Books) will be of particular interest.

3
Map and Compass Technique

Good map and compass technique is fundamental to mountain safety for no walker can be safe in the mountains if he cannot navigate accurately or understand his map. Like many skills it takes time to acquire and needs plenty of practice. It is only from gaining experience, often in adverse weather, that the walker can perfect his technique. The beginner needs a good grounding in the basics of map reading and the use of a compass which may entail classroom work or personal study followed by controlled progressive field practice.

As far as the leader is concerned, his experience must be wide so that he can navigate with precision even in severe weather conditions. However, he should also have the ability to teach the fundamentals of map and compass technique to his group so that should circumstances ever arise where, for reasons outside his control, the party became split up, individual members would be able to find their way to safety.

Map and compass technique is a very intriguing and fascinating art. A map records the historical and industrial progress of man. It may show ruins, Roman tracks and hill forts, castles, lead mines, woollen mills; it will also record the easiest routes across wild country and pin-point the dangers and difficulties to be avoided. The compass is your never-erring guide; at all times trust the information it gives you and, when in doubt as to your position, use it to accurately plot where you are and the correct course to take. The person who, in difficult country, does not use his compass and relies on 'sixth sense' navigation can either end up very tired and very lost or as a casualty statistic.

The object of this chapter is threefold: to consider the best types of maps for hill walks; to understand the Silva-type compass; and to note the techniques that are used for accurate navigation across hill country. Also outlined are suitable classroom and navigation practices that can be used to consolidate instruction.

Maps

The map is a means of recording topographical information which is gained from accurate surveys. The degree of topographical change can vary. Some areas, particularly regions of mountain or moorland, sustain very little topographical change and therefore the frequency of revision is less than for urban and industrial areas. Topographical maps are prepared in the United States by the US Geological Survey of the Department of the Interior; in Canada by the Surveys and Mapping Branch of the Department of Mines and Technical Surveys; and in Great Britain by the Director of General Ordnance Survey. The most suitable maps available for trekking or orienteering in the USA and Canada are the 1:24,000 series (1 in. to 2000 ft), 1:62,500 (1 inch to approximately 1 mile) and 1:250,000 (1 inch to approximately 4 miles). In Great Britain the Ordnance Survey series has scales of 1:1,250,000 to 1:1250. The British maps most suitable for use on hill and mountain projects are the 2½ inches to the mile, the 1 inch to the mile and the new 1:50,000 series. The Ordnance Survey 1:25,000 scale map (2½ inches to the mile) will show the best footpaths, the quickest way to a river bank and the easy or hard way up a mountain; these maps are also available covering the British national long-distance footpaths planned by the Countryside Commission (see Appendix D). The first 1:25,000 series was produced in 1945, each map covering a 10-kilometre square with contours at vertical intervals of 25 ft. A second series of maps was commenced in 1965. Most sheets cover 20 kilometres east to west by 10 kilometres north to south thus covering twice the area of the first series sheets. 1:25,000 Ordnance Survey Outdoor Leisure Maps are invaluable for the serious climber and walker. Camp sites, footpaths, mountain rescue posts, boundaries of access land and access paths are all shown plus a wealth of information given in English, French and German. Examples of maps available are the Brecon Beacons, Wye Valley and Forest of Dean, the English Lakes and Snowdonia. Other maps which have an interesting historical flavour for the walker are the 1:25,000 scale of the Antonine Wall and the 2 inch to the mile map of Hadrian's Wall. The 1 inch to the mile Ordnance Survey map is still a very popular map for the walker but the 1:50,000 series is now firmly established as the successor to the 1-inch series. The map gives an increase in scale, includes details of leisure activities and employs six colours.

The following information is normally contained on the surrounds of a map:

(a) The locality of the map.
(b) The scale.
(c) Grid reference details (where applicable).
(d) The local magnetic variation.
(e) The contour system and details of vertical interval.

(f) Conventional signs employed.
(g) Date of issue and revision

THE LOCALITY

The locality of the area shown on a map is given by the heading at the top, e.g. 'Brecon'. The index located on the bottom left-hand corner or on the side shows the adjoining sheets with hatching denoting overlaps. All the sheets noted in the index bear a number.

SCALE

The scale of a map is often indicated in three ways. Firstly by a graphic line scale resembling a ruler (Fig. 52) and giving the breakdown in miles, kilometres and less; in words, e.g. 'Scale one inch to the mile'; and by the representative fraction, e.g. in the case of the 1-inch map 1/63360, meaning 1 inch on the map equals 63360 inches in true distance, the number of inches in the mile.

For trekking purposes the 1 inch to the mile map is ideal as it gives sufficient detail and yet is compact. As previously stated this type is being replaced in Britain by the 1:50,000 series which gives greater detail. Take note that the 1:50,000 map or 1¼ inch to the mile map is also referred to as a 2-centimetre map (2 cm to 1 km); also the 2½ inch to the mile map is referred to as a 4-centimetre map (4 cm to 1 km). For orienteering training purposes the 6 inches to the mile map (1:10,560) gives much more detail than the 1 inch or 1:50,000 map but a trek of 30-50 miles would take many maps and be too cumbersome to carry. Note should be made that many of the more remote and wilder areas of Great Britain have not been scaled in the 2½ or 6 inch to the mile series.

GRID REFERENCE DETAILS

If you look at a British Ordnance Survey (OS) map you will see a mass of horizontal and vertical lines forming a pattern of squares covering the whole of the surface. On a 1 inch or 1:50,000 series

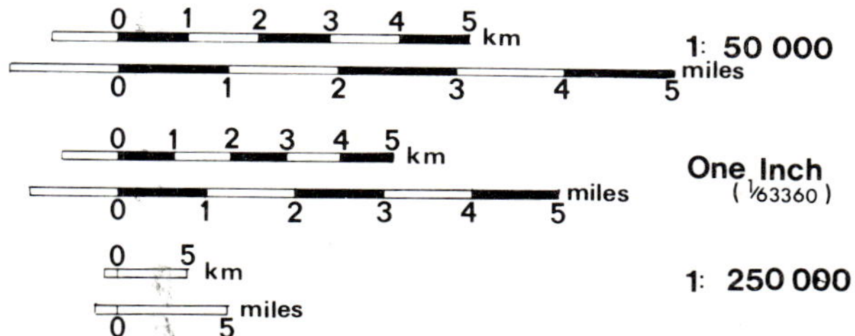

FIG. 52 Variations in scale showing the comparison between the 1:50,000 (1¼ inch to the mile) map, the 1 inch to the mile and the 1:250,000 (1 inch to approximately 4 miles) maps.

OS map these squares denote 1 kilometre and form a system of reference to any point on the map correct to 100 metres. The kilometre squares are but the smaller squares of a larger system covering the whole of the British Isles (Fig. 53) made up of a pattern of 100-kilometre squares (see also page 61). These 100-kilometre squares have grid letters and are numbered. The kilometre squares are also numbered from west to east and south to north being known as eastings and northings respectively. To give a grid reference of a place, perhaps

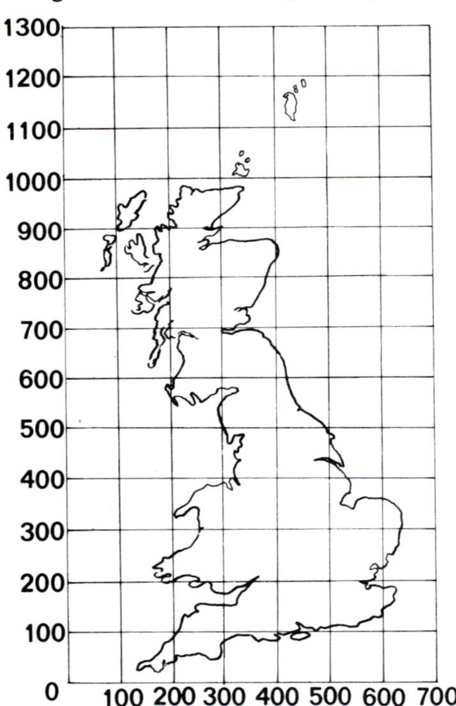

FIG. 53 The National Grid System is made up of squares of 100 kilometres.

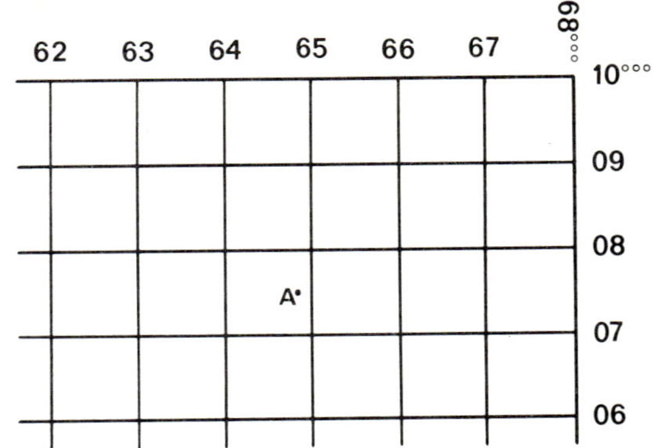

FIG. 54 Plotting the six-figure reference of point A. Take the west edge of the kilometre square in which point A lies and read the large figures printed opposite this line on the north (or south) margin = 64. Now estimate the tenths eastward = 8. Take the south edge of the kilometre square and read the large figures printed opposite this line on the east (or west) margin = 07. Estimate the tenths northward = 5. The six-figure reference of 648075 gives a reference that is accurate to 100 metres.

a bridge or church, you take the easting first, that is, you note the west edge of the square in which the point lies and read the large figures printed opposite those lines on the south or north margins. Then estimate the number of tenths eastwards (1/10 = 100 metres) and note it after your first figures. Now plot the northing by taking the south edge of the square in which the point lies and read the large figures printed opposite this line on the east or west margins. Next add to these the estimated number of tenths northwards (see Fig. 54). This is known as giving a six-figure reference and is accurate to 100 metres. It is more precise than just giving the details of the square in which a point lies (this latter system being known as a four-figure map reference). A British Ordnance Survey map also records the variation between grid and true north but this data is not really significant as all map bearings are taken from grid north as the grid lines are sufficiently close to true north to provide sufficient accuracy for navigation on foot (see page 62).

LOCAL MAGNETIC VARIATION

The needle of a compass is always attracted to magnetic north which is an area south of the north pole along the northern edge of Canada. It can be appreciated that most regions of the world are not directly south of magnetic north so that the magnetic north will, from such areas, lie east or west of the direction of true north (also see page 61). The difference between true north and magnetic north is called the 'magnetic variation' or 'declination'.

CONTOURS AND VERTICAL INTERVAL

Contours are lines drawn across the map to show land of equal height and are usually printed on the Ordnance Survey map in brown or red. The difference in height between any two lines is 50 ft in the 1-inch series and usually 200 ft on small-scale maps. This scale is known as the Vertical Interval. Take note that the 1:50,000 series map which is replacing the 1 inch to the mile series has contour values given to the nearest metre. However, the vertical interval of 16 metres is in fact approximately 50 ft. Contour lines enable us to see the height of the ground, its shape and degree of slope. Where the lines run close together the ground is steeper, where more spread out, flatter. The numbering of contour lines usually follows a rule: figures indicating height are either printed on the line, or on the higher side of it. In the 1-inch series the heights may be marked only occasionally on the 50-ft contours, but at every 250 ft there is a thicker line with the height marked. The height of any 50-ft contour can then be worked out by counting up or down from this line. You will also find small figures indicating the height at set points above sea level; these are called spot levels or spot heights.

CONVENTIONAL SIGNS

Conventional signs are those symbols illustrated on the margin of the map that serve to indicate natural and man-made features. These symbols will show types of terrain, e.g. marsh or rough pasture; water features, e.g. lakes, rivers and streams; vegetation, e.g. deciduous or coniferous forests; and habitation and development such as houses, roads or railways. Some symbols, such as footpaths and county boundaries, are quite similar so it is necessary to study the signs carefully to be able to interpret correctly the features and terrain shown on the map.

DATE OF ISSUE

The date of a map is very important as new roads, active forestation or tree cutting can soon alter the countryside and change the appearance of the area around you so that it bears little relation to that shown on a map printed perhaps only fifteen years ago or even less.

RELIEF

There are various ways in which hill and valley features may be indicated on the flat surface of a map. Contours have already been mentioned. Hachures are lines drawn down the direction of the slope. They are thicker at the top of the slope than at the bottom. Hachuring is often used on Continental maps. Hill shading is a method by which degrees of tint are used to show the amount of steepness. When the map surface is coloured, using different colours to indicate the height of the ground, the map is said to be 'layered'. For example, land between sea level and 500 feet may be shown as green with different shades at 100 feet and 300 feet; above 500 feet it may be shown to change progressively from very light to dark brown, with a change every 500 feet. Layering shows at a glance areas of high and low land and enables the shape of the mountains to be immediately identified. Form lines are a system of approximate contours made without an accurate survey and give only a rough guide to height.

HILL AND VALLEY FEATURES

By looking carefully at a map we can recognize some of the outstanding features. From our study we can note the drainage systems of streams and rivers, the exact shape of slopes and mountains and can grasp an accurate appreciation of the ground to be walked perhaps hundreds of miles away. What constitutes hill and valley features? Some of the answers are found in the following paragraphs and in Fig. 55.

Flat Land

Flat land is recognized on the map by the absence of contour lines. In hill country it may form the bottom of a valley, a plateau, the shoulder of a hill, or the top of a hill.

Uniform Slopes

A slope is uniform where the contour lines are spread equally over a distance (Fig. 55A). The steepness of the slope will be indicated by the position of the lines in relation to one another. Close lines indicate steep ground. Lines spaced well out indicate a gentle slope.

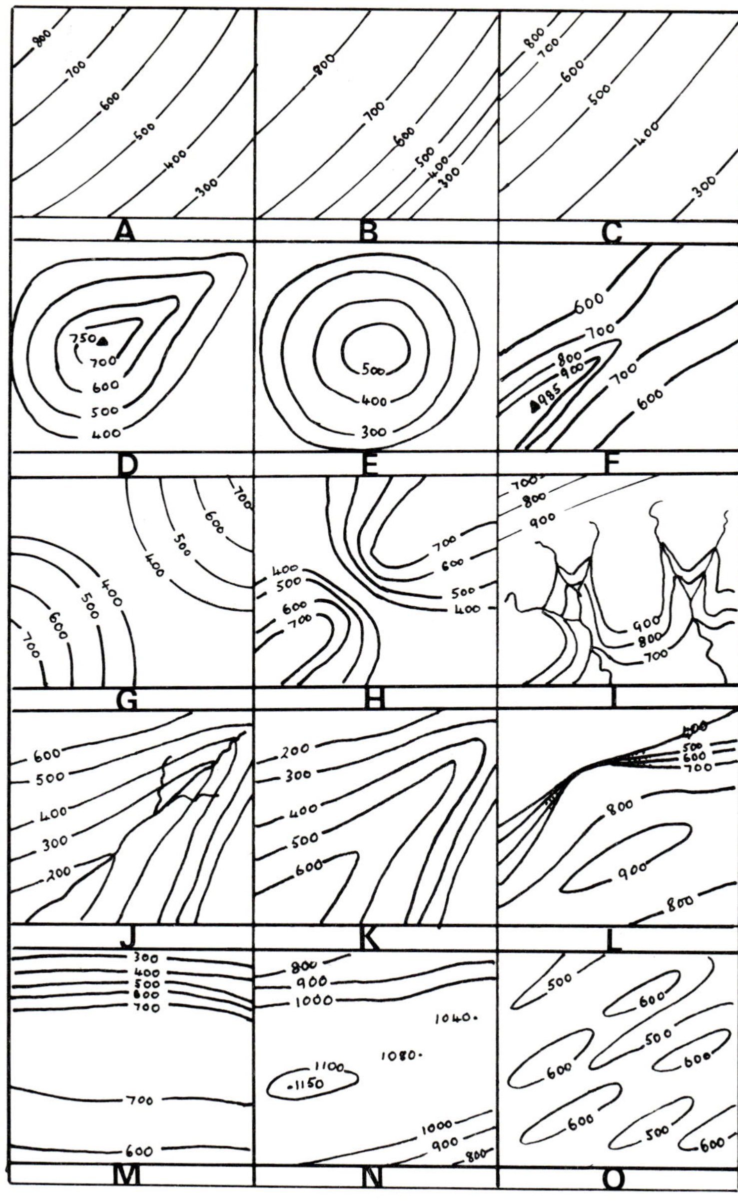

FIG. 55 Hill and valley features:
A – uniform slope;
B – convex slope;
C – concave slope;
D – hill with spur;
E – conical hill;
F – ridge with col;
G – gap;
H – gorge;
I – dissected plateau;
J – river valley;
K – spur;
L – cliff;
M – escarpment;
N – plateau;
O – undulating country.

Concave Slopes
Where there is a distinct progressive increase in the spread of the contour lines from those in close proximity at height to those more spread out on lower land it is an indication of a concave slope. (Fig. 55C)

Convex Slopes
Where there is a distinct progressive increase in the spread of contour lines from those in close proximity at a low level to those more spread out on high land the indication is of a convex slope. (Fig. 55B)

Undulating Country
Undulating country is shown as a series of contour lines of only two or three different heights but set fairly close to one another. (Fig. 55O)

Escarpments
An escarpment is a steep slope indicated by the contour lines being drawn closely together. The top of the escarpment may then fade into a long, more gentle slope on the other side. (Fig. 55M)

Plateaux
A plateau has little or no evidence of contour lines and if spread over some distance may have the height registered at certain points as spot heights. (Fig. 55N)

Cliffs
Where the contour lines run one into the other the ground will form cliffs. (Fig. 55L)

Hill Tops
Hill tops of conical hills show the contour lines roughly depicting a bull's eye. (Fig. 55E)

Hill with Spur
Where the contour lines of a hill extend out to one side the features form a spur. (Fig. 55D)

Gorges
A gorge is featured as the intersection of a mountain mass by the sudden closing of the contour lines indicating a fall in the ground to form a narrow passage through the mountain. (Fig. 55H)

Gaps
A gap is somewhat similar to a gorge except that the drop in the ground is less severe so that the slope on the mountain mass on either side is more gentle. (Fig. 55G)

Unless care is taken to practise the identification of the hill and valley features already described, map reading can develop into a hit and miss affair. Figs 55J and K show two map features which, at a glance, could be thought to be basically similar. One is in fact a valley, the other a spur. That in Fig. 55J is confirmed by the stream cutting a course down the valley. Without perusing the vertical interval figures, the other feature (Fig. 55K) could be confused with a similar valley, but with no stream. The ability to recognize all the detailed information that a map has to offer is thus very important. By careful study of the map and with practice you should eventually be able to pick out the easiest ascents and avoid difficult ground so as to select the most suitable, enjoyable route across the hills.

ORIENTING THE MAP/CHECKING YOUR POSITION

It is most important that students appreciate the need to orient the map correctly by identifying landmarks and hill and valley features on the map and relating them to what they can see locally. Without this fundamental procedure it can prove difficult to establish your position accurately and plot a correct bearing. The map must fit the landscape so turn the map so that north on the map aligns with true north. Perhaps two or more local features – a church spire, single hill or cross roads – will help you to verify your actual position and the direction of north. If you are not sure where you are it is possible to plot your position accurately by carefully observing the features around you. Find two landmarks or features that are in a *direct line* with you, perhaps a church and a single hill. Now find two more in a direct line in another direction, maybe a bridge and the edge of a wood. Plot these features by pencilling two lines on the map that run through the features. Where the lines cross is your actual position. (See page 64 for details of how to set the map by the compass.)

The Compass

There are various forms of compass on the market ranging from the cheap button-sized type that cannot be used with accuracy to the Service-type prismatic compass which is extremely accurate though expensive and fairly heavy. The Silva compass is an inexpensive, well-designed, easy-to-use compass and very popular in the field of outdoor activities.

The basic orienteering compass (Fig. 56) comprises a transparent base on which the housing is mounted. Along the top and one side of the base plate are scaled lines showing inches and millimetres so that the compass can serve as a ruler for measuring distances on a map. In the centre of the base plate is a magnifying lens to help identify small map features and, running through the lens, is the direction-of-travel arrow with an index pointer at which readings are read or set. In the corner of the base plate is a hole for the safety cord so that the compass can be hung around the neck or tied securely to a buttonhole even when kept in a pocket and thus not accidentally lost.

The compass housing is mounted on top of the base plate and can be rotated.

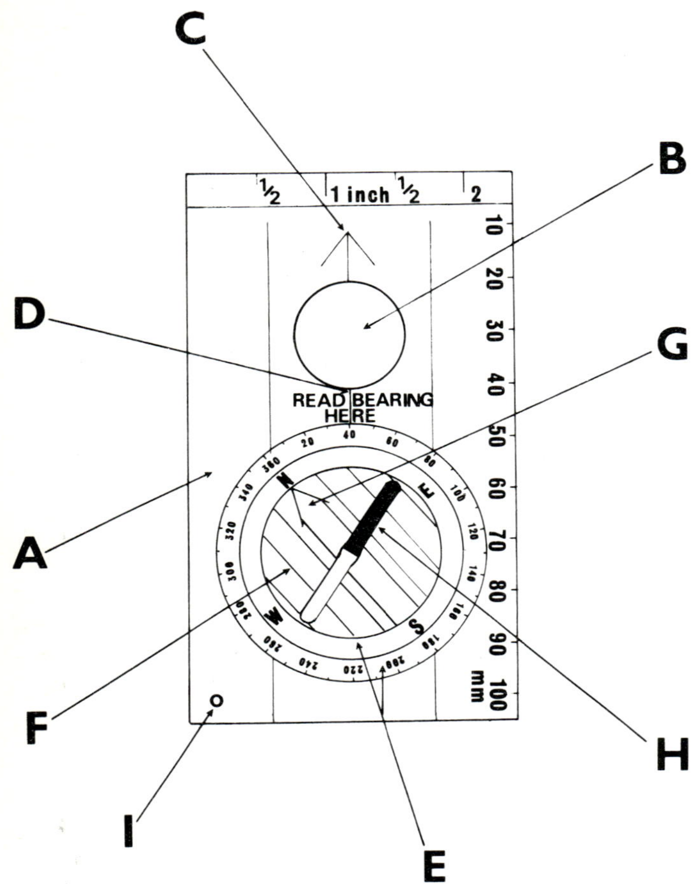

FIG. 56 Parts of the orienteering compass:
A – transparent base plate;
B – magnifying lens;
C – direction-of-travel arrow;
D – index pointer (for setting or reading bearing);
E – compass housing (with 2° graduations to 360° omitted);
F – orienteering lines;
G – orienteering arrow;
H – magnetic needle (north end is red and luminous);
I – hole for safety cord.

Its edge is marked with 2° graduations up to 360° maximum. Inside the compass housing is the transparent face which is lined with orienteering lines that are used to line up with the vertical grid or meridian lines on a map when plotting bearings from a map. It also has a large orienteering arrow that points directly to the 360° north marking. The magnetic needle swings from the centre with the luminous north end indicated in red.

Take note that the compass is extremely accurate when properly used but make sure that there is no ferrous metal (e.g. karabiner or ice axe) nearby as this will disturb the needle and cause inaccuracy. From time to time the compass should be checked to ensure its reading is constant.

Bearings

A bearing is a method of indicating direction measured through degrees clockwise from north. Briefly, there are three methods in which direction can be measured; they are:

(a) True North
This is the direction of the north pole and is indicated on the bottom or side of the Ordnance Survey map by an arrow. It is not used for orienteering in the United Kingdom as we have the National Grid System (see below and page 54).

(b) Grid North and Meridian Lines
Grid lines are lines on the map that divide Great Britain up into a rectangle of 100-kilometre and 1-kilometre squares east of an imaginary zero point set in the Atlantic west of Cornwall (Fig. 53). The multitude of grid lines running north average only about 1 or $1\frac{1}{2}°$ from true north and therefore are useful lines to refer to when taking map bearings throughout Great Britain. In other parts of the world where no grid system exists the meridian lines, which run from the north pole to the south pole, or lines drawn parallel to the meridian lines, serve to orientate the compass in relation to true north (see Fig. 58).

(c) Magnetic North
The magnetic north pole attracts the compass needle and is located about 1,400 miles south of true north in Canada in the region of the Hudson Bay (Fig. 57). The result is that true north and magnetic north coincide only along a line that runs from off the coast of Florida, through Savannah and Lake Michigan. From locations east of this

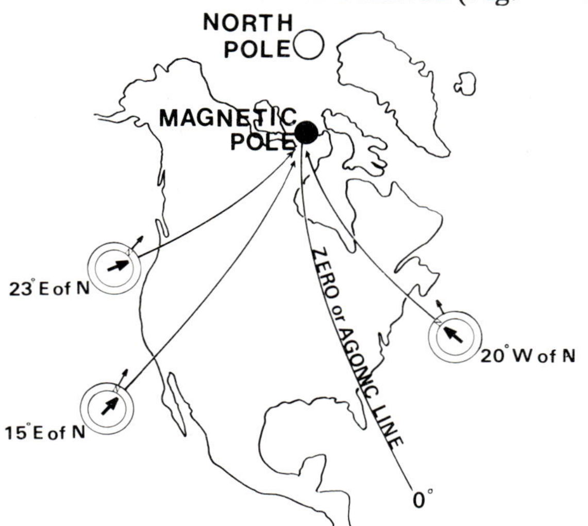

FIG. 57 The position of the magnetic north pole. The 'declination' is the angle between the direction towards which the compass needle points, magnetic north and true north. It registers west from positions east; from positions west it registers east. The diagram shows the approximate variation for regions in the USA.

zero or agonic line, such as New York, the compass needle will point west of true north towards the magnetic north pole. From locations west of the zero line, such as California, the compass needle will point east to the magnetic north pole. As previously stated, the angle between the direction the compass needle points and true north is called 'declination' and is expressed in degrees. In America the declination can vary from about 20° west in Maine to about 23° east in Seattle. In other parts of the world it also varies. In Great Britain the magnetic variation is about 7-8° west of true north. The exact variation is shown on all OS maps and varies very slightly according to the position of the area concerned. It changes very slightly each year.

As the numerous vertical lines of the British National Grid System only vary about 1-1½° from true north, the grid lines are therefore convenient reference lines on which to base readings as they are so close to the direction of the true north that for practical trekking purposes the walker in Britain needs only to concentrate on grid and magnetic north.

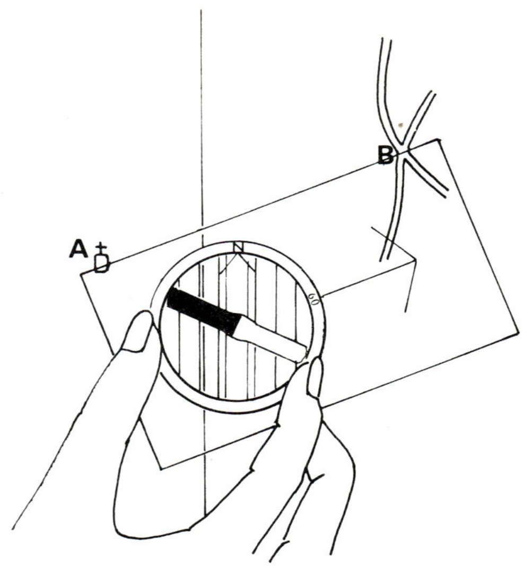

FIG. 58 Taking a map bearing. Place the base plate of the compass so that one long edge forms a line between the two points, turn the compass housing until the orienteering arrow points north to the top (north) of the map and the orienteering lines are parallel to the grid or meridian lines. Read off the bearing at the index pointer = 60°.

MAP BEARINGS

A true bearing is a bearing from true north. Grid bearings are bearings measured from the grid lines on the map. Where these lines do not exist bearings are measured from the meridian lines or parallels drawn to the meridian lines. These methods are now referred to as map bearings, i.e. those bearings taken from the map. To take a map bearing between two points (Fig. 58) place the compass so that one of the long edges forms a line between the two points. Now turn the housing until the orienteering arrow points north to the top of the map and the orienteering lines are parallel to the vertical grid or meridian lines. In this practice forget about the compass needle and just read off the bearing at the index pointer on the compass housing.

MAGNETIC OR COMPASS BEARINGS

Magnetic bearings are also called compass bearings. They are measured from magnetic north and are calculated from the map by adding the magnetic variation where the declination is west (as in Great Britain) or by subtracting the variation where the declination is east. They are also taken in the field with a compass and are sometimes called field bearings. For instance, you may see an object on the skyline that you wish to plot or determine the bearing to it. First of all keep the compass horizontal and point the direction-of-travel arrow at the object, turn the housing until the orienteering arrow is in line with the compass needle and both point north (Fig. 59). Read off the bearing at the index pointer.

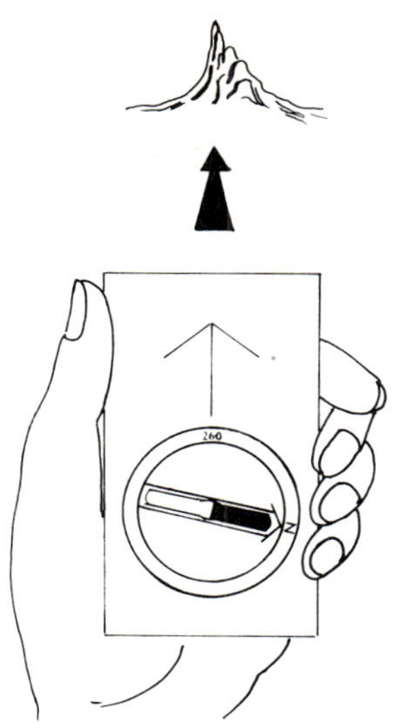

FIG. 59 Taking a compass or field bearing on an outcrop of rock. Hold the compass level then face the rock so that the direction-of-travel arrow points to it. Turn the compass housing until the orienteering arrow is parallel with the magnetic needle, the red end of which points to north on the compass housing. Read off the bearing at the index pointer = 260°.

CONVERSION OF BEARINGS – MAP TO COMPASS

Suppose, for instance, you are walking through the English countryside and wish to trek over a hill from a lake to a church and by checking the map and using the techniques described under the paragraph 'Map Bearings' you can see that a map bearing of 80° is required to bring you to your objective. Assuming that you set your compass to 80° and followed this reading accurately you would, in fact, end up some distance from your church for really you have followed a course that is 7° or so out and would have walked a course nearer 73°. The reason for this is quite simple. The compass is, of course, zeroed in Britain to a point west of true or grid north and, as stated, although there is some slight variation in parts of Great Britain we will assume it is about 7° west of grid north. Therefore a compass set at 80° on a map bearing will in fact trace a course across country that is only 73° in relation to the grid lines. Compensating for this magnetic variation is a simple affair and all you need do is to add to your map bearing the 7° variation. So, following a compass bearing of 87° will in fact keep you on the required map bearing of 80° and bring you spot-on to the church. It is very important to remember that to compensate for the declination of west as in Great Britain, when you work from map to compass and convert from a map to a compass bearing, you always add the magnetic variation. However, if the declination is east, as in the western regions of America, you must subtract the number of declination degrees from the setting.

CONVERSION OF BEARINGS – COMPASS TO MAP

Provided you know the magnetic variation for the area you are in (and this is easy as all you have to do is look at the marginal data of your map and check the date to ascertain whether there is any adjustment necessary), compass bearings can be accurately converted to map bearings and vice versa. However, to convert from a compass bearing the magnetic variation must always be subtracted if the declination is west as in Britain. For example, suppose an observer wishes to check the position of a cairn he can see and so establish that it is the correct one he wishes to walk to from the summit of a foothill. He takes a compass bearing on the point which reads as 68°. Deducting the 7° variation gives a map bearing of 61°. Using his orienteering compass set at 61° and laid on the map with one corner of the base plate on the position of the foothill, he swings the compass around until the orienteering lines are parallel to the vertical grid or meridian lines, and the orienteering arrow points north. He is now able to ensure that he is looking at the correct cairn by checking the features on the line set at 61° on the map. Take note that when converting compass bearings taken on a visual object onto a map, you subtract a westerly declination which, for example, occurs in Europe and the eastern border of the USA and Canada, and add an easterly declination which occurs in the western parts of the USA and Canada.

SETTING THE MAP BY THE COMPASS

The technique of orienting or setting the map by aligning it to features on the ground has already been explained on page 59. It is also necessary to know how to set the map with the compass for, in doing so, you confirm the identification of local features. This technique is very useful if you are on featureless moor or hill country. First of all set the magnetic variation on the compass then place the compass on the map with the side edge of the base plate along or parallel to the grid or meridian lines. The direction-of-travel arrow points to north on the map. Turn both the map and compass until the red end of the compass needle points to north on the compass housing. You now know the direction of north and the way you are facing and can identify or verify local features from those shown on the map.

WALKING ON A BEARING

Let us assume that we are going to walk from the church at A to the crossroads at B (Fig. 58). The bearing on the map taken from A to B is 60°. We note this and must add 7° to make up for the westerly magnetic declination in Britain. The drill is really quite simple:

(a) First, face the general direction you wish to travel.

(b) Hold the compass flat and turn the dial of the housing to the point where 67° can be read against the index pointer (Fig. 60).

(c) Now move the base of the compass round until the orienteering arrow in the housing is parallel with the red end of the magnetic needle and both point north.

(d) Keeping the compass flat, look down the direction-of-travel arrow and select a distinct feature to walk to, e.g. a large rock or single tree.

(e) Once you have reached that object select another in line with the direction-of-travel arrow and continue to repeat the process so that your course is accurate and straight to the crossroads at B.

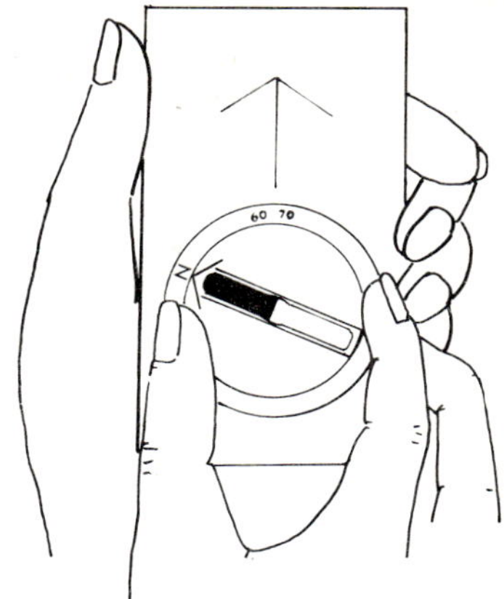

FIG. 60 Setting the compass. Having taken a map bearing between two points (see Fig. 58) you now wish to set the compass to walk from A to B. Adjust for the declination and turn the compass housing until the figure required can be read against the index pointer. Hold the compass level then move the compass around so that the orienteering arrow is parallel to the magnetic needle, the red end of which points to north on the compass housing. Point B is now in line with the direction-of-travel arrow.

It is important to select a distinct landmark to walk to. If you select, for example, a distant boulder, make sure it cannot be confused with others around it. If your course to the first object is easy with the object clearly visible all the time, you will not need to refer to the compass again until you reach that object. However, if your course is not so straightforward and you lose sight of your object from time to time, you should check your course constantly. This is done by holding the compass flat in your hand so that the north end of the needle is kept in line with the orienteering arrow. You then follow the direction-of-travel arrow. Take note that even a 1° error will ensure you are 50 ft (16 m) off course in 1000 yards (metres) and a greater error, such as 5°, can, in poor visibility, result in a vital landmark being missed; so take care and be precise when using the compass.

RESECTION TECHNIQUE

When in open country it is essential that you can trace your course accurately and, if necessary, identify your position with precision. This can be done by what is known as resection technique. Assuming that you are on an open moor (see Fig. 61) and wish to plot your exact position before camp is made and night falls. You are somewhere on the moor but can see lake C and also mountain E in the distance which you recognize on your map. These then are the points from which to take cross-bearings. Firstly, take a compass (magnetic) bearing on mountain E and adjust for the magnetic variation, which gives a reading of 56°. Now place the compass on the map so that the side of the base plate intersects the top of mountain E. Keep the edge of the plate on point E and without disturbing the setting, swivel the entire compass on the map until the orienteering lines are parallel with the meridian or grid lines and the orienteering arrow points to north on the map. Pencil a line on the map along the edge of the compass from E to F. Your position is somewhere along this line. Now repeat the same procedure by taking a compass bearing

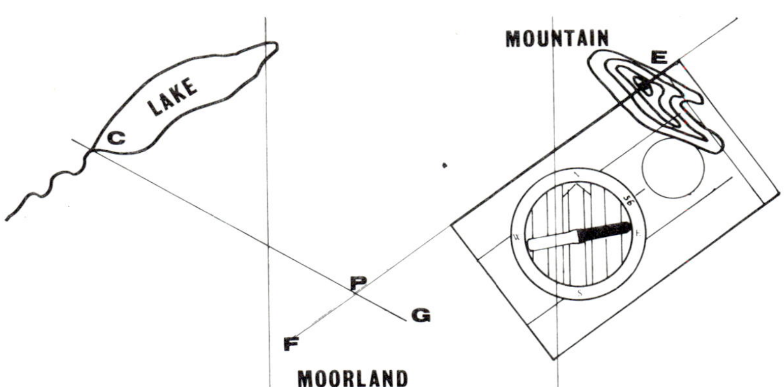

FIG. 61 Resection technique enables the walker to prove his position from identifiable features or objects in the distance. Take a compass bearing on E, convert it to a map bearing, place the compass on the map as shown with the orienteering lines parallel to the grid or meridian lines. The orienteering arrow points to north on the map. Draw the line E – F. Similarly take a compass bearing on the corner of lake C and convert it to a map bearing; place the compass on the map as above then draw the line C – G. Your exact position on the moor is at P, i.e. where the lines cross.

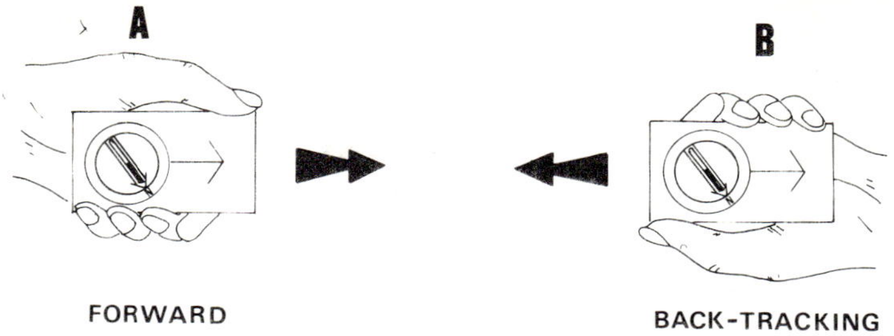

FIG. 62 Back-tracking: A – how the compass is normally held to follow the direction-of-travel arrow; B – how it is held, reversed, to back-track over the same course by sighting along the reversed direction-of-travel arrow.

on the edge of lake C and convert it to a map bearing then place the compass on the map. When you have drawn the line C-G from the corner of lake C, the two lines will intersect giving your exact position at P. You can now make camp with the knowledge that even if the morning is foggy or misty you know exactly where you are and can plan your course accurately to the next rendezvous.

BACK-TRACKING

There are times when you need to back-track your original course. Perhaps you have realized that you have overshot a landmark and must return along the same route for several hundred yards to pick up a path. To retrace your steps accurately you can add 180° to the compass setting if the original setting was below 180° or subtract 180° if the setting was above 180°. A much simpler way is to use the compass with the same setting: on the original course you held the compass with the direction-of-travel arrow pointing away from you towards the original destination (Fig. 62A), so to return along the same course hold the compass with the direction-of-travel arrow pointing *towards you* instead of away from you (Fig. 62B). Orientate the compass by turning your body until the north of the compass needle points to north in the compass housing. Locate a distinct landmark in line with the reversed direction-of-travel arrow then walk to that landmark. If necessary, repeat the process with other landmarks and your original course can be retraced accurately. By using this method there are no degree figures to subtract or add, therefore no possibility of errors in calculation, and no adjustment to the compass is required; you simply use the compass backwards. The practical application of this technique is not confined to the walker – back-tracking with a compass can also be employed by huntsmen when in dense forests. After shooting a deer it may be necessary to get help to move the animal. The huntsman will mark the location of the deer with something that can be seen at a distance, such as a large white handkerchief tied to a branch. He may set his compass in the direction of a track that leads to a hunting lodge then set off and pace out the distance until he reaches the track. When he has obtained assistance he will return from the same point on the track with the compass set as before but now used backwards as described above. The huntsman will check off the correct number of paces so that he is aware of the exact distance to where his prize lies.

NAVIGATING AROUND OBSTACLES

There are occasions when an obstruction, such as a swamp, boulder field or rocky outcrop, will require you to change course and walk around the obstacle. If you can see across the obstruction and can spot a prominent feature such as a single large boulder in line with your bearing, walk around the obstruction and continue with the bearing from the boulder. If necessary, double check that you are on the right track by taking a back-bearing to the point you came from. This can be done in the two ways described above: firstly by re-setting the compass and adding 180° if the reading is below 180° or subtracting 180° if the reading is above 180°. The direction-of-travel arrow should then be directly in line with the point you came from. The second and easier way to check your position involves holding the compass so that the direction-of-travel arrow points towards you instead of away from you (Fig. 62B). The compass must be oriented so that the north of the compass needle points to north in the compass housing. Look back down the direction-of-travel arrow and the point you came from on the other side of the obstacle should, if you are in the correct position, be in line with the shaft of the arrow.

If you are not able to see across the obstacle or pick out a prominent feature in line with the correct bearing you must use another method to ensure that you do not go off course as you walk around the obstruction. In this case it is best to

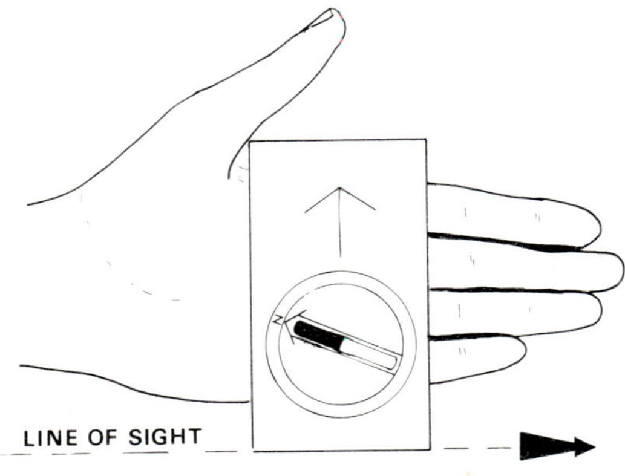

FIG. 63 Pursuing a course at a right angle without altering the compass setting. To turn off at a right angle from your original course hold the compass as shown and make sure that the orienteering arrow is parallel with the compass needle, the red end of which points to north on the compass housing. Now sight along the rear edge of the base plate. (See also p. 69 and Fig. 64.)

navigate by a series of right angles and by pacing out parts of the detour. You have the choice of re-setting the compass or using it with the original bearing. In the first instance add 90° to the compass setting for a turn to the right, or subtract 90° for a turn to the left, then pace out the distance to clear the width of the obstacle. Now re-set the compass to the original course until the obstacle is passed on your left (or right), then re-set the compass again by adding (or subtracting) 90° so that you pace back until the point reached is in line with the original compass course. The compass is again re-set to the original course and you can proceed on your journey. In the second method the obstacle can be cleared and the original course accurately pursued without any alteration to the compass by using the base plate as a sighting line (Fig. 63). Firstly, hold the orienteering compass crosswise in the hand with the compass orientated in the usual manner so that the red needle points to 'N'. Now sight along the rear edge of the base plate to a suitable landmark clear of the obstruction (Fig. 64). Walk to the point counting your steps as you go. Now hold the compass in the usual way (Fig. 62A), and follow the direction-of-travel arrow and walk far enough beyond the obstacle to clear it, then stop. Repeat the technique of sighting along the edge of the base plate but in the opposite direction and count

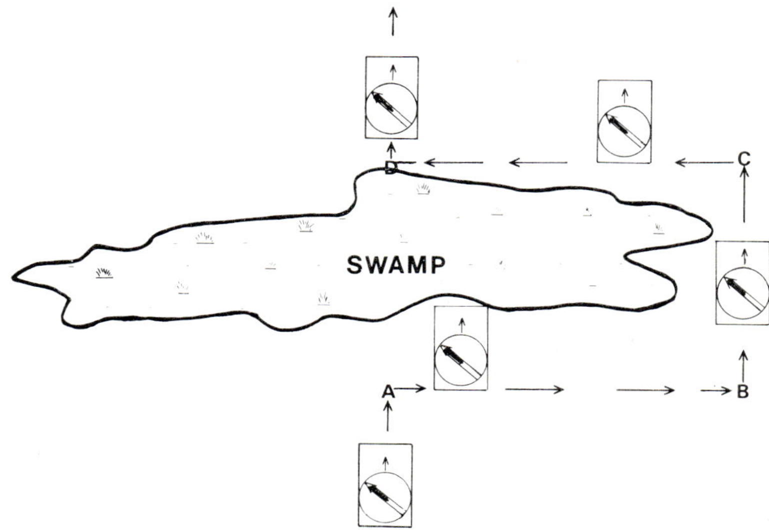

FIG. 64 Navigating around an obstacle. The compass is used on legs A – B and C – D as described in Fig. 63. Don't forget to pace out the distance from A to B, then count the same number of steps back from C to D.

out the same number of paces back to a point that will be in line with the original course. Now proceed on that course by following the original compass setting.

Teaching Map and Compass Technique

If properly taught, map and compass technique can be a very interesting subject for both pupil and instructor alike. Initially it is best to introduce a group to the use of the map and compass in the classroom. If ample suitable desks or tables are available, maps can be unfolded, features read and distinguished, and grid lines noted in conditions that permit maximum concentration. If this sort of instruction is given outdoors and the wind and weather conditions are unsuitable it can become difficult for the group to readily assimulate the information. Thus, in most circumstances, the classroom is a much better environment for initial map instruction. The instructor should use whatever visual aids are available, such as relief models of terrain and maps of the same area. As much interest as possible should be stimulated and comparisons of old maps, aerial photographs and modern maps will help generate this interest. The lesson can be further enlivened by reference to Gaelic place names and their meanings, followed by the identification of such names on the map. Ideally, it is best to relate what can be seen on the map to the immediate surroundings, but this, of course, is not always possible if the school or club is located in a built-up area. Photographs or drawings of ridges, escarpments or saddles relating to the features on students' maps can be shown with the aid of an overhead projector. In this way it is possible to bring home to the student and into the classroom the actual shape of features giving him a vivid impression of the true outlines of a specific mountain in relation to the maze of contour lines on his map.

An appreciation of the significance of contour lines is fundamental to the understanding of maps and any teaching medium that will help explain contour patterns should be employed. A simple illustration of contour lines can be given by dipping a rock part-way in water. The water line is marked then the rock submerged one inch deeper and the line is repeated and so on until the top is finally covered. Viewed from above the rock is patterned with lines that, by their proximity, indicate the steepness or gentleness of its sloping sides. Another method of explaining contour lines is to use half a turnip or large potato sliced at regular intervals to show the pattern of contour lines that can then be noted from the side and from above. Visual aids as shown in Fig. 55 will assist pupils to appreciate gradients, concave and convex slopes, spurs, escarpments, valleys and other hill and mountain features.

When teaching compass work the instructor may wish to add further interest and refer to ancient compasses and the magic needle of the Chinese. Use a blackboard and drawings to explain points of the compass and bearings. When explaining magnetic, grid and true north, stress that as the numerous vertical lines of the British National Grid System are close to the direction of true north, for practical trekking purposes the walker in Britain needs only to concentrate on grid and magnetic north. However, for other parts of the world where no grid exists the instructor will need to emphasize the use of meridian lines aligned to true north or lines drawn parallel to the meridian lines. The Silva compass should be explained in detail; if need be, using a large plastic demonstration model or large drawing to do so. Once its use is understood, intensive classroom practice should be carried out using the compass to measure bearings on the map. Progress to using the compass out of doors to take bearings on features and then identify those features on the map. This will involve the conversion of compass (field) bearings to map bearings and the verification of the features located by the compass with those on the map. Other exercises should comprise taking a bearing from an object on the map, converting this to a compass bearing and setting this bearing on the compass. It should be emphasized that when carrying out resection technique using the Silva-type compass there is no need to convert the bearing taken to a back-bearing when plotting it on the map. However, this conversion may be necessary with other types of compass.

With practical experience students should eventually be able to select the best route on a map and know how to make out route cards with estimates of the time a walk will take according to Naismith's rule (page 88). They must also be taught to identify and note escape routes off a mountain. Class work should therefore include such items as identifying six-figure map references, applying Naismith's rule between two given points, and route selection for simple trekking projects. Students should be required to note suitable 'legs' for a walk (page 89), work out map and compass bearings for the legs and to select possible camp-sites and emergency bivouac points, such as a ruined farm house, that are identifiable on the map.

It must be appreciated that indoor practice must not be considered a substitute for outdoor map and compass practice but it does add meaning to a teacher's explanation of the use of the compass, particularly so if no immediate practice is possible out of doors and lessons are carefully thought out and well presented. However, the progression to the taking of bearings off such features as trig points and cairns in hilly areas will be easier as the basic principles will then have already been understood in the classroom under ideal learning conditions. There is therefore much to practise both in and out of doors. The following paragraphs are aimed at providing the instructor/ teacher with some indoor and outdoor practices in order to consolidate information already given to students.

INDOOR PRACTICES

(a) Grid Reference

Students are called upon to identify a feature at a given map reference.

(b) Symbols

The instructor calls out the name of a symbol and the students find that symbol on their maps and also give the six-figure map reference. Another method requires the students to draw the symbol named.

(c) Basic Compass Practice

Students are called upon to note the bearing with their compass of various features in the room, e.g. the door handle, corner of the far window frame, the clock, etc.

(d) Taking Map Bearings and Setting the Compass

The instructor gives a six-figure map reference for a distinct feature which the students identify on their maps. He then gives a series of references for other features; students trace these and, with the use of the compass, note the map bearing of each feature from the first. These bearings are finally converted to compass bearings.

(e) Distance

Pupils copy the scale rule from their map on to the edge of a piece of paper or card. The instructor then calls out the names and locations of two different points and students carefully check the direct distance between the points. This practice can be extended by also asking the students to work out the height to be climbed on a walk between these points.

(f) Contours

The instructor tells the group that they are at a set point on the map and then asks questions which relate to the contours in the area, such as: Does the road run uphill or downhill? Which way does the stream run, north to south or south to north? Is it a slow-moving or fast-running stream? How steep is the hill to the east? What type of slope exists to the south-east, concave or convex? etc.

(g) Map Sections

Students are given two six-figure references then called upon to draw the cross-section of the ground between the two points to show concave and convex slopes, escarpments, plateaux, etc.

(h) Appreciation of Terrain

The instructor gives four reference points and students are required to describe the ground between these points in great detail noting footpaths, marshland, types of slopes, types of forest, ruins, farms, etc.

(i) Route Selection
Two points on a map several miles apart are given to students. The instructor then requires the group to work out the best route between the points and to divide the walk into 'legs' (see page 90). Students are called upon to record the map and also compass bearing for each leg and to consider the time it would take to walk each leg using Naismith's rule and allowing for height climbed, weight carried, and distance involved. Additional exercises can be added by noting possible escape routes that may need to be used in the event of bad weather and also areas suitable as possible bivouac sites.

OUTDOOR PRACTICES

(a) Taking Bearings
From a central point students are required to note the compass bearing of predominant features, e.g. a distant farm, a village church, etc. or, if in a confined area, the school clock or the corner of the school wall.

(b) A Compass Training Walk
This walk is a simple exercise aimed at consolidating initial instruction in the use of the compass and stressing the need for fine accuracy. A student places a marker on the ground at his feet, such as a twig or coin, and then, by walking on a series of bearings outlined below, he should succeed in navigating himself back to his starting base (Fig. 65). First of all, he sets the compass for an arbitrary direction anywhere between 0° and 120° and, for the purpose of this example, selects 50°, walks 40 steps on that bearing and stops. He then adds 120° to the original 50°, making 170°, and re-adjusts the compass. He walks 40 paces on the new bearing and stops. He once more adds 120°, so the compass bearing reads 290°. After a further 40 paces, if his navigation is correct, the marker should be between his feet for he has walked the sides of an equilateral triangle. The exercise can be repeated as above but starting with a different degree setting somewhere between 0° and 120° and then adding 120° as each point is reached.

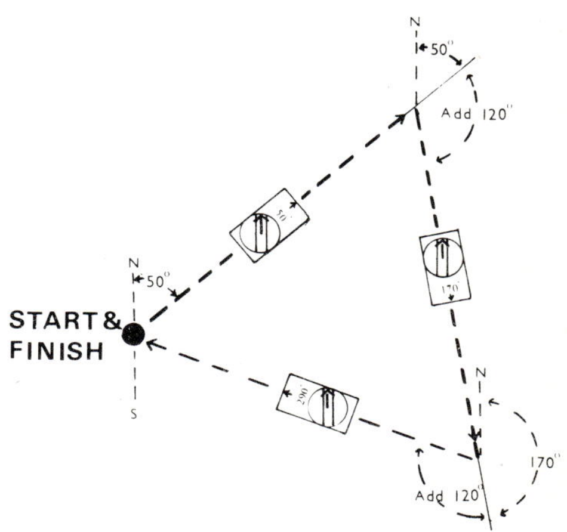

FIG. 65 A compass training walk.

(c) Miniature Orienteering Course

A miniature orienteering course may cover only a few hundred yards of woodland yet will give excellent experience in walking with the compass without any risk to novice participants. It can also provide an enjoyable competitive element. The course comprises a series of numbered markers attached to trees and each marker gives the compass bearing and distance in paces to the next marker. The participants start either singularly or in teams of two at two-minute intervals and the fastest around the course is the winner. The course is easy to arrange and can serve as valuable initial training.

ORIENTEERING COMPETITIONS

Orienteering calls for a full understanding and the precise use of the map and compass. The orienteer must know how to read a map and recognize symbols and contours. He must be able to solve swiftly and accurately problems of direction, terrain, and speed. The course planned by the organizer demands an intelligent approach from the participants in order to attain the series of check points between the start and finish lines in the quickest and most economical way. Orienteering therefore requires the basic fundamentals of good compass work, the ability to interpret correctly the terrain shown on the map and a full appreciation of your own physical ability – all factors which are closely related to expedition trekking in the hills. These factors, plus the enjoyment orienteering offers, make it a suitable subject for inclusion in a modified form in a pre-expedition programme of training. The rules for the sport of orienteering are rather detailed but the forms of competition outlined below have been simplified for expedition training purposes. The area selected for an orienteering course must be safe with no dangers such as marshland, cliffs, loose rocks, etc. Ideally it should comprise gently undulating ground, be partially wooded and have a start and finish point in close proximity. Dotted around the course will be control points that must be found by competitors and, for the purpose of a training course, these can comprise white cloth patches or football corner flags and flag posts. Different coloured pens tied to a bough at each control point can be used to mark competitors' cards with a special letter clearly indicated. If additional map and compass practice is to be introduced the organizer can call upon competitors to recognize and record features on set bearings from a number of control points, or carry out a resection on a certain leg and record the bearing taken. Marks for accuracy are then awarded. Each person will need a 2½ in. to the mile series map sealed in a protective polythene cover, a route card, pencil and compass. Dress will depend on the terrain and the time of year. Basketball boots give good protection to the ankles and a tracksuit worn over a rugby jersey will give a great deal of protection from cold, branches and thorns.

The following simple team competitions stimulate a lot of interest as individuals can contribute to the result of their team:

(a) Clover-leaf Competition

This competition has a central combined start and finish point and the course follows the outline of a clover leaf. In a six-'leaf' event the competition may be organized so that each twelve-man team will provide two persons to cover each leaf and then hand over the map and compass to the next two for their leg. Each of the six 'leaves', which are legs of the relay, may have two or three control points, the route to these points being at the discretion of the competitors. A staggered start time of one- or two-minute intervals will initially help to spread out the competitors.

(b) Score Competition

A large number of control points, perhaps in the region of twenty, are shown on a master map and each person will record these on his own map. Each of these points carries a scoring value, the nearest to the start and finish area being perhaps 5, the furthest being perhaps 50. The object of the competition is for each two-man team to visit as many of the controls as is possible in the time allowed for the competition. Members of teams that are late back to the finish are penalized by having points deducted, e.g. 10 points per minute. It is very important that competitors have sufficient time after the briefing to work out carefully the points to be visited in order to get the most out of the experience of competing. They have to decide if they will attempt the difficult controls or the more simple ones, the bearings from one control to the next, the distances involved, and the estimated time at a jogging or walking pace.

All teaching schemes for map and compass work should aim to provide interest and enjoyable progressive training because accurate map reading and precise navigation make for confidence and added safety.

4
Planning an Expedition

Expedition dangers can be unpredicted dangers – a sudden dense mist, an unexpected deterioration in the weather, an ice-covered ridge path, illness of a member of the group. The aim when planning an expedition is to reduce these possible dangers to acceptable levels and to do so requires the careful preparation of the individual, his equipment and the selection of a project which is within the competence of the group.

When planning an expedition the leader should consider several important factors. These include age, experience of the group (particularly so of the less able), size of the party, individual fitness, equipment available, degree of difficulty of terrain, length of the walk and forecast weather conditions. Planning and leading an expedition requires skill and an intelligent approach. Trekking the hills does not embrace the same thrill as a white-water canoe tour or a cross-country ski expedition, so special care needs to be taken to stimulate as much interest as possible. To get the most out of a walking project the leader needs to do his homework first and obtain interesting data of the area in which the group is to walk. Projects may have a historical aim such as tracing the position of Roman hill forts and roads, the location of crashed World War II aircraft on a range of hills, or a geographical aim such as finding the precise location of the source of rivers in an area. Botanical schemes can also be considered where the types of flowers and vegetation at various levels on a mountain range are noted and recorded; such projects all add considerable interest to walking expeditions and can give that extra motivation and enjoyment. The leader should include group members in the planning phase and select the most interesting route that is practicable so as to aim to obtain maximum interest from the scenery and the environment.

The Leader

The leader should be a person well experienced in mountain walking, energetic, determined, sympathetic, cheerful yet cool in adverse conditions such as bad weather or an emergency. The degree of practical experience he requires is not easy to define in precise terms as so much depends on what is to be undertaken and at what time of the year. The United Kingdom Mountain Leader Training Boards provide a comprehensive scheme for the training and the certification of mountain leaders and instructors. They run a basic Mountain Leader Training Scheme (Summer), plus the Instructors' Certificate and Mountain Instructors' Advanced Certificate. The Mountain Leader Training Scheme (Summer) is intended to cover minimum competence in the technical skills required to take a party on walking and camping expeditions on British mountains under normal summer conditions. Brief details are shown in Appendix B. As indicated in the preface, this book is aimed at providing leaders and potential leaders with information that will assist in planning and leading basic hill-walking expeditions in temperate climates under summer conditions.

The basic qualities of leadership are innate. No two leaders will be the same for leadership has purely individual qualities that cannot be acquired just by training or by study. However, the person who possesses the desirable attributes of leadership plus high technical skill and experience will be the most competent. Leadership involves inspiring within your group a sense of trust, co-operation and confident team work. It is therefore not a position to be allocated or accepted lightly.

It is extremely important that the leader:

(a) knows the ability of his group and can identify the stronger and weaker members;
(b) is able to appreciate the feelings of the individual to each situation and is sympathetic to any apprehensions he/she may have;
(c) keeps a close watch on the physical and mental condition of his charges;
(d) is able to maintain good morale in bad weather conditions and in difficult situations.
(e) plans each day's activities with a definite purpose but, should weather circumstances alter, he must be flexible and prepared to amend the programme accordingly;
(f) is able to quickly recognize danger and avoid hazardous situations;
(g) is a good organizer and covers all necessary pre-expedition preparations, the expedition itself and the arrangements back to base, so ensuring that the group is well looked after at all times, both on and off the hills.

Your aim therefore as a leader should be

to stimulate as much interest and enjoyment as is possible from the adventure of walking in the hills and mountains, at the same time ensuring that your charges are not exposed to hazardous situations.

Basic Planning

SIZE OF THE PARTY

In any mountain walking party the actual ratio of people to each leader is an important factor. As long ago as 1960 Lord John Hunt, renowned mountaineer and leader of the British expedition to Everest in 1952-53, stated: 'In easy mountain terrain it is not possible for an experienced adult to supervise more than ten novices; where the grade is more difficult, the maximum ratio may be as small as one in three.'

The number in a party needs to be very carefully considered in the light of a variety of factors. So much will depend on the difficulty of the route, the experience of the participants, their age, physical condition, the length of the expedition and expected weather conditions.

It is dangerous to take large parties of perhaps fifteen to thirty persons into remote hill country for it is often impossible for one person to control a large group in easy terrain let alone more exacting country. In addition, it is not easy for the leader to give detailed instruction to a large group and interest can be lost. Should a mishap occur in the hills or the weather change suddenly for the worse the risk to a large party can be considerable, and in a large party the difficulties can easily multiply.

Hill-walking groups should therefore not exceed ten persons and not comprise less than three; six is ideal for most hill treks for the overall management of the party is straightforward, close supervision by the leader is also easy and the numbers are favourable for instructional purposes. However, take note that when an expedition has to cover difficult country which involves some steep ground and the requirement to rock scramble or ridge walk, the numbers should not exceed six. A minimum number of three persons is necessary for the simple reason that if an accident does occur to one of the party a second member can stay with that person to render first aid and arrange shelter while the third goes for help. Also, the number should be restricted to three persons if there are numerous lengthy areas of difficult ground to be covered en route which will require the leader to use the safety rope frequently and give very close supervision.

INDIVIDUAL ABILITY

The length of each day's walk and the total duration of an expedition should depend very much on the ability of the people taking part. Individual ability can be related to age, physical fitness, experience and motivation. Age is one of the factors that should influence the physical effort expected of individuals. Ambitious, long, continuous walks of 20 miles (32 km) per day for boys or girls about the age of sixteen or even older, carrying their camping equipment, can result in considerable physical strain being imposed on the walkers. This will apply even if they are very well prepared for the project. Therefore, about 8-10 miles (12-16 km) per day over mountainous terrain will provide adequate exercise before all enjoyment is lost and the journey becomes just one long slog.

Similarly, 10-15 miles (16-24 km) each day is a good distance for those in their late teens and older. Bear in mind that the physical effort involved in carrying a load 10 miles (16 km) in true mountain country cannot be compared with walking on the flat and requires considerably more energy. The weight of equipment to be carried is very important. It should not be necessary for the load to exceed 40 lb (18 kg). However, as a guide the total load for a camping and trekking expedition should never exceed one third of the bodyweight of an adult. For young people 30 lb (13.6 kg) is the accepted absolute maximum.

It may be argued that young people in their late teens can walk more than 15 miles (24 km) each day and those younger, more than 10 miles (16 km). However, it is better, if to err at all, to err on the right side and underestimate rather than overestimate ability. In the former case the party is not put at risk and the rendezvous point (RV) is reached early giving more time to put up tents, cook a meal, relax in the late afternoon and start fresh on the next day. In the latter case, at best, this can make for a late arrival at the RV, with a tired party and, as tiredness is cumulative, it will be carried on into the next day. At worst, the acute fatigue of one or more members could bring the expedition to a halt and result in a casualty.

A sound basis of physical fitness is highly desirable. Optimum performance is obtained from individuals and the group where experience, sound fitness and strong motivation are the combined factors.

Equipment

The personal and camping equipment required for walking projects should vary in accordance with the type of expedition planned. The project may comprise a low-level or high-level base camp from which daily training treks are to be made. In this instance there may be no requirement for walkers to be heavily laden but, nevertheless, protective clothing and also emergency cover and rations should be carried just in case of a sudden change in the weather or if an emergency situation develops. The height above sea level at which a project is planned, the time of year, and the forecast weather conditions must influence the amount of protective clothing to be worn or carried. Low-level projects are defined as those planned below 1,500 ft (455 m). High-level projects are defined as those planned above 1,500 ft (455 m). This is an arbitrary delineation for it must be stressed that as weather conditions can vary so much at all heights, plans for high- and low-level projects often need to be flexible. A walk may be planned as an expedition perhaps covering 40-50 miles (60-80 km) of isolated low foothills or even higher terrain. Such an expedition needs to be completely self-contained and prepared for any reasonable eventuality. On the other hand, if a low-level base camp is to be set up from which treks are made, the organizer is not confined to using lightweight equipment at the base and greater flexibility may also be possible with supporting facilities. Cooking shelters, toilet tents, larger base tents and a greater variety of rations can be used which could not be feasible at a high-level camp, nor on an actual expedition. A mountain walk requires weight to be kept to the minimum and, as previously stated, it is recommended that the load should not exceed one third of the bodyweight of adults and 30 lb (13.6 kg) for young people. Outlined in Appendix C are the items required for summer low- and high-level day walks and summer low- and high-level expeditions.

Food

ENERGY

A young person carrying a load of about 25-30 lb (11-13 kg) over 15 miles (25 km) of rough terrain will use up a considerable amount of energy and over 4000 calories per day will be necessary to sustain such effort. To meet this energy output an increase of at least 25 per cent in his normal intake of food will be required. Hard physical activity burns up calories at an alarming rate and a mountain ascent with a pack can produce a calorific requirement of 500-600 calories per hour. Such effort over 80 seconds uses the equivalent of the energy produced from one lump of sugar which would normally meet the calorific requirements for one hour when resting. It is important that persons taking part in long and hard walking projects are sustained by adequate energy-giving food so two hot nourishing meals should be taken each day in order to replace energy used up. A good quality balanced diet that contains plenty of carbohydrates and protein to provide 4000-plus calories is necessary. It should include a high-energy snack at mid-day, perhaps accompanied by a mug of hot, sweet tea. If an expedition is to last for many days it is all the more important that rations are well balanced. About 10 per cent of the food should be protein, e.g. meat, fish, eggs, cheese, milk, cereals and nuts;

about 15 per cent should be in fats such as dairy produce, fat, meat and nuts. Carbohydrates such as sweet stuffs, bread and potatoes should constitute the remainder of the diet.

WEIGHT

There are several points to note when planning food supplies for a walking project. A person normally consumes about 3 lb (1.3 kg) of food per day which, on a long-distance trek, can add up to a fair weight. It is therefore necessary that food selected for use on an expedition is as light as is practicable but the content should give the required energy output. With careful planning it is possible to reduce expedition rations to about 2 lb (1.1 kg) per person per day. In order to keep weight to a minimum, if it is possible, plan the route of an expedition through a village or hamlet every second or third day so that supplies can be purchased for a couple of days at a time. Whatever the form of project envisaged, whether it be a six-day trek across the mountains or a two-day walk across the moors, the use of light and compact food packages is important.

The average walker wants to make practical and economical purchases, if possible from a local supermarket or village store. He cannot afford expensive, custom-produced survival-type food packs. I have therefore outlined below the types of foodstuffs that are widely available on the market and also indicated how some can be used. The selection of the items will depend largely on the leader's and group's choice. If a base camp is established storage and cooking facilities should be available for a greater range of foodstuff than would normally be carried on a walk and will permit a greater variety of menus.

VARIETY

Most foods contain a large proportion of water, but if dehydrated their weight is reduced by 80-90 percent. The original weight and bulk is quickly regained in its preparation when water is added to the food. It is possible to obtain a variety of convenience meals pre-packed in dried form. Some are based on textured soya protein such as pasta vegetable bolognese, savoury risotto, rice and curry, vegetable stew. Preparation consists of merely adding boiling water and the meal is ready to eat after 5 minutes' hydration. These meals are light to carry, give large tasty portions and are cheap to buy. Examples of other foods that can be obtained in dehydrated form are carrots, turnips, onions, beans, potatoes, milk and soups.

To give an idea of the comparative quantity of dehydrated food before and after it is reconstituted a packet of dehydrated potato will weigh 12 oz (340 g) but, when prepared with water added, will make a total of fifteen servings.

Similarly a packet of onion flakes may weigh 1 oz 10 dr (45 g) in dried form, but when the flakes are prepared and added to stew, soup, curry or mince they equal ¾ lb (340 g) of prepared onions. Thick dehydrated soups are good purchases. A 2 oz 15 dr (85 g) packet of country pea soup with herbs and spices added makes 1¾ pints (1 litre) of soup. The simmering time required is 15 minutes. There are also other thick varieties retailed such as tomato, vegetable and beef, leek, and chicken noodle soups. However, packet soups can be dual purpose; that is, they make an excellent soup but also, when other foodstuffs are added, constitute a light meal. Country pea soup can be made into a Bavarian-type dish by adding frankfurters in ½-inch slices, stirred into the soup. If additional body is required in a soup add noodles or rice and this will make for a thicker and more filling dish. Many soups require only 5 minutes' simmering which is important if cooking fuel is limited. To keep weight to a minimum it is better to carry only the meat basis for your main meal in its original constituted form, such as minced beef, corned beef, steak, etc., to which can be added dehydrated vegetables, such as potatoes, peas and carrots.

A nourishing breakfast makes for a good start to the day. Swiss-style breakfast cereals, made up of fruit, wheat, oats, nuts, raisins, brown sugar and skimmed milk, provide a filling breakfast or snack, give much nourishment and can be taken with cold or warm milk, evaporated milk or even honey. Instant porridge oats are ideal for colder conditions. These are easy to prepare – just pour boiling water or hot milk on to the oats with sugar or salt as required. There are several types of powdered milk on the market which can be added directly to coffee or tea so fresh milk is not a necessity. Vacuum-packed bacon will keep for several days if kept cool. When cooked with fresh eggs it makes a welcome change on the breakfast menu, but dried eggs can also be used. Crispbreads or fresh brown bread will keep longer than white bread. Pumpernickel, which is a form of German sliced black bread, is normally sold in foil and is a good purchase as it will keep for a long time.

Tube foods are worth noting for they not only add flavour to a meal, but also are light in weight. Cheese spread, tomato purée, meat paste, fish paste, mustard, jam and marmalade are sold in this form and give that extra taste to a meal or snack. An old favourite for flavouring is that small cube of Oxo that gives a delicious aroma to meat dishes; it also makes a most enjoyable warm beverage, which is so welcome if you have trekked many hours over the hills on a cool late-autumn day. Six cubes take up little more space than a box of matches.

If a lightweight stove is to be used as the sole means of cooking it is important to check the menus planned against the amount of fuel that can be carried. If fuel is limited, then meals that need lengthy warming processes are out. On the other hand, your cooking stove can be augmented by a cooking fire if the site is suitable and natural fuel readily available. Such types of meals would then be quite feasible.

EMERGENCY RATIONS

In the interests of safety, reserve rations such as barley sugar, chocolate, glucose tablets, mint cake, dried fruit, which all have a high calorific value yet have little bulk or weight, should be carried and always kept in reserve in case of an emergency.

Lastly, whatever is to be purchased for the daily menu must appeal to the appetites of the walkers. Food must be as attractive and appealing as field conditions will allow, but with a little thought extremely good nourishing meals can be prepared over even the smallest of burners. Think out menus carefully, weigh foodstuffs and, if necessary, 'field test' some meals at home. What Napoleon said about an army marching on its stomach can also be applied to hill and mountain walking. Good food is important to sustain fitness and morale.

Preparation and Training

There is much more to the organization of a walking project for young people than the issuing of equipment followed by the embarkation of the group into the hills, and the commencement of the actual trek. It is extremely important that novices and those with little outdoor activity experience are first given pre-camp instruction on living in the wilds, the use of equipment, basic map and compass technique and safety procedures. The overall success of an expedition will be measured in the personal achievements of individuals and the satisfaction they gain from applying skills previously learned in pre-camp instruction. A lack of such instruction resulting in bad camp-craft can have a very detrimental effect on morale and the degree of success of the project. Insufficient knowledge of how to put up a new or unfamiliar tent can, on a cold wet evening, cause delay and unnecessary discomfort. Similarly, a poorly pitched tent which has its flysheet touching the tent roof can, in bad weather, result in a leak and the occupants losing sleep because of damp bedding. Insufficient knowledge about how a paraffin pressure stove works may result in a cold breakfast or a delayed start to the day. A lack of sleep, cold meals, and general discomfort are the ingredients for low morale which, under adverse conditions, can undermine the safety of the group. However, sound pre-camp instruction makes for confidence and comfort.

CAMPING TECHNIQUE

When dealing with novices the main

aspects of camping that should be covered with lectures/demonstrations as appropriate are as follows:

Use of Equipment

TENTS
- types of
- pitching
- striking
- care of

RUCKSACKS
- types of
- packing
- carrying
- emergency use of

SLEEPING BAGS
- types of
- care of

STOVES
- types of
- maintenance of
- burning time

UTENSILS
- types of
- use of
- use as containers
- methods of cleaning

SAFETY AT CAMP
- cooking in and out of tents
- lighting fires
- fire precautions

Camp Knowledge and Techniques

SITE SELECTION

HYGIENE
- water supplies
- food protection and storage
- camp cleanliness
- personal cleanliness

CAMP FOOD
- types of light-weight food
- ideas for menus

COOKING TECHNIQUES

FIRES
- cooking fires
- small camp fires

BASIC KNOTS AND LASHING

CAMP ORGANIZATION

THE COUNTRY CODE

MAP AND COMPASS TECHNIQUE

A basic understanding of map and compass work should be acquired by all before an expedition sets out. It is true that with good weather and a suitable area it is possible to give such instruction under field conditions. However, as previously stressed in Chapter 3, the classroom is normally a better environment for initial map and compass instruction, certainly much better than a wind-swept hillside, though progress should be made to outdoor work as soon as is practicable. The main aspects of map and compass work to be covered are:

Use of the Map

Types of map
Marginal data
Conventional signs
Scale

Methods of showing relief
Contours
Topographical features
Setting the map without the compass
Navigation with the map alone
The grid system
Four-figure reference
Six-figure reference
Measurement of distance and speed (Naismith's rule)
Route planning

Use of the Compass
Types of compass
Map bearings
Compass bearings
Setting the map by the compass
Back-bearings
Resection technique

SAFETY

A walking party that has been well briefed and instructed in the fundamentals of camp-craft, map and compass work and mountain safety procedures is a confident party. If such a group is subjected to difficult conditions they will be aware of the procedures that the leader may call for and know how to apply the techniques required. On the other hand, should a group that has not had such instruction be overtaken by very bad weather when crossing an open moor, the conditions will certainly not be ideal for the leader to instruct the group in bivouac construction so as to ensure their safety. Far better if the group have already been taught the basics of bivouac construction and have even constructed their own shelters using a thick polythene sheet and the protection afforded by a depression in the ground, a sheep wall, or an outcrop of rock. Similarly, it is important that individuals have a basic knowledge of the effects of stress on the body and know the causes, symptoms and treatment for exposure; also, that the body needs a greatly increased water intake during long hard exercise and that thirst is a poor indication of the body's requirements (see Chapter 5). All this type of information adds up to one important factor – the safety of the individual and therefore of the group. Naturally, to instil so much information depends on the time available for pre-expedition instruction. It is also very necessary that the leader instructs with tact and skill so as not to over-dramatize the dangers of hill walking. Ideally, novices should be instructed in the following mountain safety topics and the leader should revise such aspects with those who have some experience of hill trekking:

essential equipment
emergency clothing
bivouac construction
signs and treatment of exposure
effects of heat
elementary weather forecasting
navigation by natural means
accident procedure
first aid

To cover all aspects of safety and procedures relating to hill and mountain walking would itself require a detailed course run in a suitable location. Such aspects as river crossings, movement on steep ground, etc., as amplified in Chapter 5, would not normally be included in pre-expedition instruction given to novices, for the terrain they would be attempting should not possess such difficulties. Nevertheless, if an emergency situation arises where such difficulties are encountered and cannot be avoided it is essential that the leader can effectively apply the techniques that will ensure his group is able to overcome the hazard and continue to easier, safer ground. As a group gains experience there is considerable merit in gradually introducing the party to such activities as rock scrambling, the use of the rope on steep ground, a simulated river crossing. Such techniques will add interest, prepare novices for more advanced projects and make the group more capable and confident in an emergency. However, if taught, it is stressed that the leader must be competent to demonstrate, instruct and supervise such techniques.

TRAINING WALKS

Walking parties should, wherever possible, comprise small numbers – as already explained, large groups are difficult to control, limit the instruction possible and lower the safety margin. Each member of the group should be given set responsibilities (see below) in order that he or she can get the most out of the walk and contribute to the safety of the party. The leader should stress the following points so that each group member is aware that he is responsible for:

(a) assisting with planning the route, noting the map and compass bearing, the distances between RVs and the estimated time each leg of the walk will take, and recording these details on his own route card (see page 90 and Fig. 68);
(b) continuously taking notice of the surroundings and making use of his map and compass so that he is aware of the precise location of the party and can, under the leader's supervision, take over the lead position in the column if called upon by the leader;
(c) if nominated as the rearman, keeping his position at all times. He is then responsible for ensuring that no-one gets left behind and also alerts the leader if the party is becoming strung out;
(d) keeping with and not straying from the group when on the trek;
(e) keeping his equipment in a clean and serviceable condition.

Normally the leader will lead a group of novices from the front to ensure correct navigation and to select the most suitable ground to walk; the other members will follow in crocodile style behind the leader. They should keep a suitable distance of a few paces between each other to observe the ground immediately ahead and avoid uneven ground or pot-holes. They must not become strung out, which is a common tendency with novices, particularly when they become tired. However, the position the leader adopts can vary and may depend on the experience of the group and the circumstances at the time. In dense mist or fog he may decide to lead from the front if the experience of the group is limited; the next most experienced member will bring up the rear. In other circumstances the leader may wish to position himself in the middle or even at the back if he has an experienced deputy to lead the party.

Walks should be planned so that if possible each trek will be a little harder or longer than the previous, yet always incorporate specific training values. Each training walk should therefore have a clear aim, perhaps to include selected techniques. These techniques can range according to terrain and weather conditions from navigating for a period using the watch as a compass (see page 142), building emergency bivouacs during a break or practising the principles of crossing a river in spate using the rope across a dry ravine (see page 116). Perhaps the leader may, at a predetermined point, simulate a casualty situation on a steep, though safe, slope. With the aid of the safety rope he can demonstrate the principles of belaying onto a rock and tying a triple bowline to fit as a sit sling around the waist and each thigh of an experienced member of the party (see Fig. 80 and page 106), then lower him down the slope in the sling to the supposedly injured person (see pages 106 and 104). The sit sling is transferred to the 'casualty' and both are recovered by the instructor. Other practices can include simulated casualty situations calling for the construction of a Piggott rope stretcher (Fig. 102) the use of one- and two-man carrys over a short distance (Figs 96-101). However, carrys would only be practised when there is no possibility that the group could be unduly fatigued, particularly so if they are still some distance from their final RV.

ROUTE PLANNING

Accurate route planning from the map is based on the ability to correctly interpret the relief indicated by the pattern of the contour lines and also the symbols shown on the map. In order to fully appreciate the wealth of information on a map it is necessary to study with considerable care the various symbols and features shown. However, let us assume that you have obtained from a close study of the map a good picture of an area of hills and now wish to consider the best course across the hills from a start point to a final RV. The best course

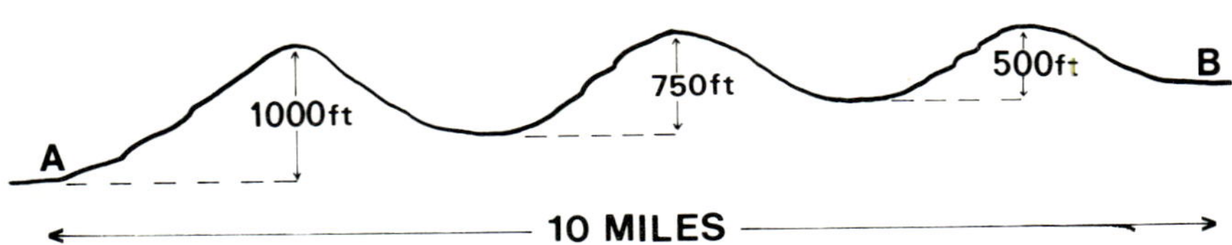

FIG. 66 The application of Naismith's rule. The distance from A to B is 10 miles (16 km) which would take a walker carrying a full load 4 hours at a speed of 2½ mph (4 km/h). In all 2250 ft (675 m) will be climbed at a rate of 750 ft (225 m) per half hour which will require a further 1½ hours. The journey from A to B without stops, would therefore take around 5½ hours.

across the hills is rarely the most direct and the following principles need to be considered in your planning:

(a) note the easy way to gain height to commence the actual route across the hills, thus avoiding any very hard ascents;

(b) once height has been gained, plan to maintain height even if this does incur a reasonable detour. It should be borne in mind that energy used to regain height lost in pursuing a direct course is often much greater than that used in a moderate detour which maintains height;

(c) plan to avoid hazards such as narrow ridge walks, or cliffs, or possible difficulties such as an unbridged river;

(d) note how the walk can be divided into legs from one distinct feature to another, such as from a ruin to the confluence of a stream, from the stream to a cairn, etc.;

(e) check the approximate total distance of the route selected and also the legs using the graphic scale line on the map. (Bear in mind that the longer the leg, the greater the possibility of an error in navigation, particularly so in bad weather.)

The route should be planned so that the group is on easy ground or in a valley well before nightfall and, in order to do so, you need a means of estimating the time it takes to cover varying terrain. W. Naismith, founder of the Scottish Mountaineering Club, evolved a sound method of estimating time required to cover distance and height. His formula is based on a speed of 3 mph (5 km/h) for an adult carrying no equipment, or 2½ mph (4 km/h) with camping gear. To this you add half an hour for each 1000 ft (300 m) climbed unladen, or 750 ft (225 m) if laden (Fig. 66). Take note that the speed of young people should always be planned at 2½ mph (4 km/h) and a half hour for each 750 ft (225 m) climbed. This formula does not take into account rest periods, forced reductions in speed due to bad weather, or the effects of fatigue. If roads or good tracks are included in the plan then the estimated speed over such ground should be 4 mph ($6\frac{1}{2}$ km/h).

Having satisfied yourself that the overall distance is well within the capability of the group and sufficient daylight is available, even allowing for bad weather conditions that could slow down and delay the arrival of the party at the final RV, the leader should now work out the legs of the trek. These are the individual sections of the walk that together comprise the overall trek and are planned to ensure a constant accurate course across the hills and moors. The more featureless and open the country, the greater the need for accuracy. The length of each leg selected should be fairly short and made from one distinct, easily identifiable point to another, e.g. from a cairn to a trig point (trigonometrical pillar) or small lake. The actual length will depend on the type of ground to be covered; in difficult country or in bad visibility the leader would be justified in splitting the walk up into legs of a few hundred yards; in easier terrain and in good visibility the legs could be a mile or two. However, remember that the longer the leg walked on one bearing the greater the possibility of a naviga-

FIG. 67 A training walk. The walk is divided into legs from one distinct feature to another. A map bearing is taken from one RV to the next then converted into a compass bearing. Naismith's rule is then applied to work out the approximate time required for each leg. All these details are recorded on the route card (see related route card, Fig. 68).

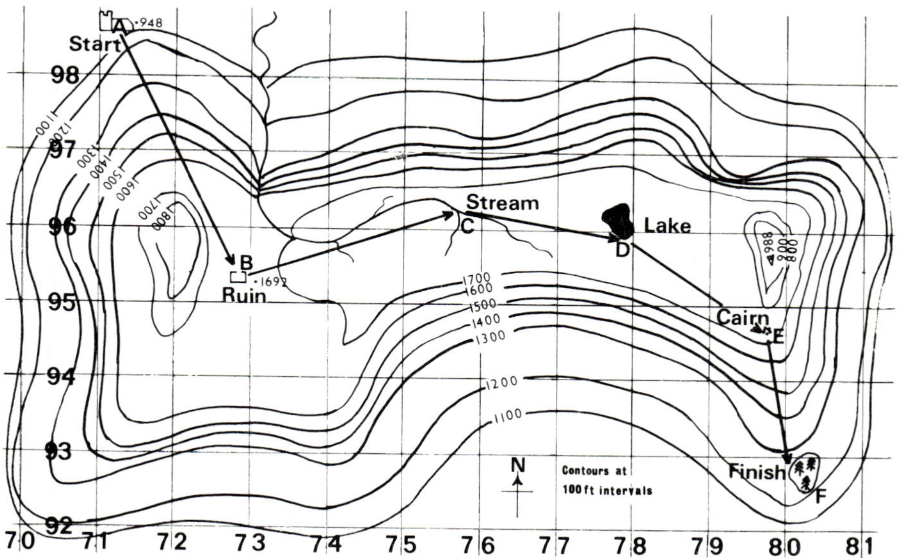

tional error. A 1° error will put you off course by 50 ft (16 m) at 1000 yards (metres). A 4° mistake will throw you off course by 200 ft (60 m) at 1000 yards (metres). The same error of 4° will ensure that you are 400 ft (120 m) out at 2000 yards (metres); which is more than sufficient to miss the RV completely, particularly so if the visibility is reduced or the ground is uneven so that the trig point or small lake cannot be seen.

Let us assume that the leader is planning a training walk to traverse a range of hills from point A to F, perhaps over a distance of about 9 miles (14.5 km) (Fig. 67). With the involvement of the group he has planned the route carefully to take in the most suitable walking ground and divided the walk into legs. The map bearing of each leg, from point A to point B, from point B to point C, etc., is now taken and converted to a compass bearing and recorded by the group on their route cards (see Fig. 68). To eliminate the possibility of a mistake the map bearings and compass bearings are re-checked. By applying Naismith's rule the approximate time for each leg is worked out. If the party is heavily laden and the distance from A to B is 2½ miles (4 km) with an ascent of 750 ft (225 m) the approximate time to cover that distance will be 1½ hours without stops. Similarly the distances between the other RV points on the trek are checked and the approximate time it should take between each RV point is also calculated and recorded on the route cards. Recording information in this way can be invaluable – there will be no need to work out map bearings and convert them to compass bearings on the exposed summits perhaps in driving rain and with the wind trying to tear the map away. The correct map and compass bearings from each RV will have been already checked and re-checked and the information is readily available sealed neatly in a polythene transparent cover together with the map. By knowing the approximate time it will take between RVs, should the weather become misty or foggy, the leader will also know when to commence a detailed search for the ruin or cairn concerned and should not walk past an RV. Having selected the good weather route, should the leader consider it prudent, it may be necessary to work out and record a bad weather route that will follow lower and less-exposed ground even if the route is not so convenient as the original good weather route. If weather is suspect the leader should examine the map with great care to locate features that could afford shelter such as a derelict hill farm, a ruin, or a protected valley or ravine that could, by their position, offer shelter from strong prevailing winds. If need be, the party could bivouac at these points until the mist clears or a storm blows itself out. He should look also for good escape routes off the mountain, such as paths and safe escarpments, and note the general direction that streams run so that if necessary they can be

ROUTE CARD

FROM CHURCH **Map ref** 713986

OBJECTIVE WOOD **Map ref** 801929

LEG	START POINT	MAP REF	TO (RV)	MAP REF	MAP BEARING	COMPASS BEARING	DISTANCE /CLIMB	ESTIMATE OF TIME	DEPT. TIME	ARRV. TIME	REMARKS
1	CHURCH	713986	RUIN	729953	154	161	2½ miles + 744 ft.	1½ hours			
2	RUIN	729953	STREAM	757963	70	77	2 miles	48 mins.			
3	STREAM	757963	LAKE	778959	100	107	1½ miles	36 mins.			
4	LAKE	778959	CAIRN	798947	125	132	1½ miles	36 mins.			
5	CAIRN	798947	WOOD	801929	170	177	1¼ miles	30 mins.			

DATE: 26 MAY 1978 **totals:** 8¾ miles + 744 ft | 40 mins, 4 hrs. 40 m. | : ADD REST PERIODS SUNSETS: 2105 hours

WEATHER CONDITIONS

WIND

		BECOMING
FORCE/ SPEED	LIGHT SCALE 1 (1 – 3 M.P.H.)	MODERATE BRZ. SCALE 4 (13 – 18 MPH)
ESTMD. AT HEIGHT	AT 1500 – 2000 ft. SCALE 2 (SLIGHT BRZ 4 – 7 M.P.H.)	AT 1500 – 2000 ft. SCALE 6 (STRONG BRZ 25 – 31 M.P.H.)
DIRECTION	VARIABLE	NORTH-WEST

CLOUDS

		CHANGING TO
TYPE	CUMULUS	NO CHANGE
HEIGHT	BASE AM. 1500 ft.	BASE P.M. 5,000 ft.

TEMPERATURE

		BECOMING
SEA LEVEL	18°C (64°F)	NO CHANGE
ESTMD. AT HEIGHT	APPROX 12°C (53°F) IN SHELTERED POSITION AT 1500 – 2000 ft.	NO CHANGE
LEVEL OF FREEZING	NOT APPLICABLE	

FORECAST OUTBREAKS OF RAIN, CONDITIONS BECOMING BRIGHT WITH SUNNY INTERVALS AND SHOWERS, TEMPERATURES NEAR NORMAL

ESCAPE ROUTES

ROUTE 1			ROUTE 2			ROUTE 3		
START POINT	RV	BIVOUAC POINT	START POINT	RV	BIVOUAC POINT	START POINT	RV	BIVOUAC POINT

FIG. 68 A route card (front and back views) showing how the journey outlined in Fig. 67 is planned with the route divided into legs. The back of the route card can be used to record details of forecast weather conditions and, according to terrain, possible escape routes.

followed to safer, lower ground. Streams usually find the quickest way down a mountain but care needs to be taken to ensure that in doing so precipitous ground is not encountered. Usually when following a stream, the most suitable descent will be down the shoulder of the mountain or hill that encloses the stream.

As previously stated, it is important that everyone on the expedition knows the route planned and, if possible, has taken part in the planning. Each person will have located and drawn the route in pencil on his map and also worked out the map and compass bearings from each RV to the next. These bearings should be checked by the leader. Each person should also be aware of the possible escape routes and bivouac points. The object of this study is to add experience and interest to the walk and show how to plan and enjoy mountain walks in safety.

NAVIGATION IN BAD WEATHER/ DIFFICULT COUNTRY

The compass provides the most exact means of navigating in the hills no matter whether the conditions are good or bad. If visibility is poor, such as when dense mist or cloud descends, its use is essential. The compass will provide a wealth of information if properly used; observe, trust and apply this information. Some of the techniques of navigating in bad weather or in difficult terrain are outlined below.

In bad weather with limited visibility or in areas of heavily forested terrain it will be necessary to follow the direction-of-travel arrow for considerable distances with the compass held in front of you as you walk (Figs 60 and 62A). Be especially observant in those conditions and study the map carefully in relation to the ground. Small features in mist will look bigger than they really are and it can be difficult at times to tell whether you are on level ground or a slope. When contouring slopes in a dense mist there is a tendency to lose height without realizing. However, an increase of air pressure on the ear drums can sometimes indicate to the walker that he is in fact walking downhill. If you are walking a path which is shown on the map, watch out for known recorded features such as a nearby trig point or a junction with another path which is sometimes marked with a large cairn of stones. When in mist or featureless country no suitable landmark may be distinguishable in line with the desired compass bearing. However, a party of three can maintain the correct direction by walking in line with about ten paces between each person. The last walker carries the compass and directs the party by keeping the lead man in line with the centre walker. Any deviation by the lead man may then be corrected by instructions from the last person, e.g. 'two paces to the right', 'one pace to the left', etc. The use of route cards with an estimate of time required from one RV to another can be extremely useful in bad weather conditions (see page 91, Fig. 68). Supposing the distance over a moor to a cairn marked on the map is half a mile, using Naismith's formula of 3 mph (5 km/h) for an unladen walker (see page 88), this distance should take approximately 10 minutes to cover. If it is not possible because of mist to locate the RV after 10 minutes the leader should halt the party and recce each direction by walking a set number of paces on a bearing and then reverse the bearing back to the party (Fig. 62) and repeat the procedure until the cairn is located. It may be necessary to carry out several such sweeps from points on the original course before the cairn can be found. If not already known the map bearing to the next RV is then noted and the bearing converted to a compass bearing. The distance to the RV is checked and the approximate time required to cover the distance worked out. The party then sets off confidently into the mist knowing the correct bearing, distance and approximate time to the next RV point, which is perhaps a small lake. When that RV is reached the process will be repeated to the next RV. As already stated, when walking a planned route it is best to have previously noted the map bearing and worked out the compass bearing from one RV to the next, also the distance and approximate time it will take to cover the leg.

When in thick mist the compass can be used to carry out a survey of the area you are in. First of all pick out an easily recognizable feature, such as a lone boulder or turf pond, then walk perhaps 100 paces east, then 200 west, to take you right through the central point before returning 100 paces back to your starting point. If the track you are looking for has not been discovered repeat with 100 paces north, 200 south and then 100 back to the central point. In this way you are ensuring that even if you fail to find the required track you will not go any further off course. Another way to examine the ground around you is to walk a set distance perhaps 100 paces north, 100 east, 100 south and then 100 west back to the central point before walking 100 paces south, east, north and then do the final 100 paces west back to your boulder or pond. Similarly, two 100-pace squares to the west can be covered from the central point to encompass and check the whole of the area.

In good or bad visibility you may, at times, come across obstacles in your path such as a difficult boulder field, a deep ravine, a mountain lake or area of marshland. For a while it will be necessary to change direction and alter course. It is important, particularly so in fog or mist, that when you change direction you eventually return to the correct course and employ the techniques described on page 68 and shown in Fig. 64.

Many of these bad-weather techniques can be initially practised in good weather conditions but take note that skills and techniques are really put to the test when conditions have deteriorated to such an extent that visibility may be nil and individuals are under stress. The more practised in navigation the more confident a walker is to deal with such situations. There is no substitute for practice and experience.

Walking Technique

BASIC TECHNIQUE

The conservation of energy is extremely important when hill trekking. The aim is to acquire an easy effortless walk. The body should lean slightly forward to offset the weight of the rucksack. There is little movement of the arms and the hands are kept free. The legs are allowed to swing forward into a comfortable stride. High knee movements and over-striding are to be avoided as they are very fatiguing because the body has to re-adjust its position with each foot movement. The pace should be steady and rhythmical and the feet placed down with a deliberate step. As each stride is made the whole of the foot comes into contact with the ground, rolling from the heel to the sole. If the ground surface is rough look for level spots to place the foot and so reduce effort and also strain on the ankles. When a group starts off on a walk the pace should be steady and never too fast, thus energy is conserved for difficult parts of the trek or for an emergency should it occur. The leader must check that the pace is based on the slowest members in the party. Weaker members should be placed immediately behind the lead man and should never be allowed to trail. Where possible, the pace used on flat ground should be maintained on moderate gradients, but the length of stride may be reduced for steeper and more undulating terrain, then lengthened for slight descents and easy ground.

ASCENTS

In order to conserve energy it will be necessary to reduce the pace on very steep slopes and go into a steady 'lower gear'. Each step is made more deliberately to get the best support and, where possible, the whole surface of the boot placed on the ground. This can be achieved by placing the heel on a firm tuft of grass or small rock. It is often necessary not only to reduce speed when a steep climb is being made but also the angle of ascent to the slope. The leader should lead the group in a slow diagonal zig-zag course across and up the slope rather than pursue a direct ascent. In this way the weight of the body is taken on the outside of the left foot and the inside of the right if the ascent is to the right. As you change to traverse diagonally up to the left, the weight is distributed onto the outside of the right foot and the inside of the left. In order to attain a summit directly above the original commencing point at the foot of the mountain the diagonal zig-zags need to be as equal in each direction as is possible. There is often the temptation to rush the last few yards to the apparent top of a mountain slope. However, these 'tops' sometimes prove to be false crests and the actual top is still hidden from sight. It is best, therefore, to keep in a steady lower gear and not increase the pace – there can be a long way to go and several such ascents. At all times energy should be conserved. There is no point in making a non-stop ascent up a steep slope if, in doing so, the effort exhausts some of the group: far better to make several short stops on the ascent and arrive at the top ready to stride on.

DESCENTS

Steep descents need to be tackled with care for the weight and strain put on knee and ankle joints as well as on thigh muscles can be considerable, particularly if the walker is heavily laden with a full pack. Avoid overstriding and placing the foot down heavily as the body can be jolted and control lost. In some instances it is desirable to zig-zag down a slope but with the knees slightly bent to offset any jolting. Select a firm place for each foot, dig the heels well in to keep the foot as horizontal as possible, and place the toes on any firm projections to help reduce the weight on the toes and any rubbing of the skin occurring.

TYPES OF GROUND

The surface of a mountain or moorland can vary considerably. Short grass is a pleasant and easy surface to walk on and is normally the safest surface for an ascent or descent, but wet grass slopes need to be treated with care as they can be very slippery. In summer, areas of bracken should, if possible, be avoided as it makes for difficult and laborious walking and, after a shower, can soak you from the damp leaves and also be very humid. Bracken is unsafe as a handhold on rocks and hillsides as it is very brittle and the roots come away easily. Large areas of bog and marshland are normally indicated on the map and should be avoided. At the extreme it can be dangerous to attempt to cross areas of bog or, on the other hand, progress across marshland can be severely restricted and boots filled with cold water and black mud, making the going very tiring. Deep heather makes for hard walking as the feet have to be lifted high with each step so it is also best avoided. The easiest surface to walk on is that of a track and these are normally marked on the map though they rarely go the way you want to. Sheep tracks can prove useful but, if you come across one that seems to run your way, frequently check with the compass the direction in which you are travelling as it is easy to turn off route unconsciously. Sheep tracks are much narrower than man-made tracks and deeper, so don't confuse the two. A scree slope is the name given to an area of mountain debris made up of loose stones or boulders. These slopes are often found where the contour lines indicate a steep escarpment. If the scree is made up of stones no bigger than about 3 ins (75 mm) across it can serve as a rapid way down the mountain provided the whole of the slope can be seen and it does not end in a vertical drop. If the slope comprises larger stones there is the possibility that the surface could avalanche and injure someone below. Scree running is fun but must be closely supervised and the party deployed in a shallow arrowhead formation so that if stones are dislodged there is no possibility of injury to a member of the party. Boots should be worn to avoid damage to the ankles and the descent is made with the legs stiffened and the heels dug well into the scree. Generally speaking, it is better to avoid scree altogether when carrying a very heavy pack and it should always be avoided in high or remote places where even a twisted ankle could have serious consequences. When ascending an escarpment it is advisable to walk up grassy slopes and avoid areas of scree as it is normally too loose to give good support.

RESTS

If you are heavily laden rest for about 10 minutes per hour; if lightly laden, about 5 minutes. It is, of course, extremely difficult to attempt to give an exact rest period for it will depend on the individual's or group's fitness, the type of country and the weather conditions. When you decide to stop, select a place out of the wind if you can, where the area ahead of you can be seen. Thus while you loosen your laces and relax you can trace out the route and relate it to your map. Make full use of these stops. Have drinks from your Thermos or brew some hot, sweet tea but avoid eating large meals during the walk - it is better to eat a little reasonably frequently and, as a general rule, sweet foods give the most energy. Re-adjust your pack and cover any sore parts on your feet with zinc-oxide plaster. If your feet are very tired immerse them in a mountain stream - it works wonders as it is tremendously refreshing.

Walks and Projects

Young people learn from using their initiative and by experiencing the responsibility of leadership. They are often adaptable, determined and relish the challenge that outdoor activities offer. Suitable training that fosters interdependence and initiative should, whenever possible, be included in schemes.

Provided the group have been carefully instructed and prepared there is considerable merit in their planning and carrying out an expedition through easy hill country on their own. But it must be stressed that potentially dangerous country must be avoided and the leader should satisfy himself that such projects are within the capability of his charges. Some expeditions and training schemes suitable for young people are outlined below.

Appendix D gives details of the long-distance footpaths or bridleways planned by the British Countryside Commission, some of which cross isolated hill terrain and are suitable for basic expedition training purposes. The Ordnance Survey have 1:50,000 and 1:25,000 maps of these areas. Ordnance Survey maps, including those covering the footpaths planned by the Countryside Commission, can be obtained in large towns from local stockists. The Ordnance Survey main agents for England and Wales are Cook Hammond & Kell Ltd, 22-24 Caxton Street, London SW1H 0QU.

The Duke of Edinburgh Award scheme makes provision for bronze, silver and gold awards for boys and girls taking part in expedition schemes on foot. These grades range from a two-day trek over 15 miles (24 km) and one night camping out to a 50-mile (80-km) trek over four days with three nights camping out. Further details of the Duke of Edinburgh Award can be obtained from the Duke of Edinburgh Award Office, 5 Prince of Wales Terrace, London W8.

The Ten Tors Expedition, across the wilds of Dartmoor, is an annual competition for young people. Teams of competitors are required to navigate to ten nominated tors (distinct outcrops of rock) on Dartmoor. Various routes are laid down by the organizers and must be covered in 34 hours which includes a compulsory 10-hour overnight rest. According to age, routes vary from 35-55 miles (56-88 km). Details of this competition can be obtained from: The Secretary, Ten Tors Competition, G Training, Headquarters South West District, Bulford Camp, Salisbury, Wiltshire.

5
Hazards of Mountain and Moorland

Isolated hills and moors can provide a challenge for the hill walker and a form of exhilaration that cannot be found in other forms of outdoor activity, for such areas have a beauty, majesty and mystery of their own. Remote high terrain can, at times, present certain difficulties for the walker that need to be avoided or, if necessary, overcome. These can vary in type and severity and range from steep ground, swollen mountain streams, snow and ice on high ground, electric storms, to the insidious effects of cold, fatigue and wet that add up to that dangerous and sometimes fatal condition – exposure. However, with knowledge and correct technique dangers can be avoided and difficulties overcome.

Steep Ground

When planning a hill-walking project avoid very steep ground especially where novices are concerned. Long, grass slopes can tire even the fittest if they are very steep and the expedition is carrying a reasonable amount of kit for a several-day trek. Some steep slopes and descents can give rise to apprehension if the group members are not used to heights or are new to hills. It must be stressed that it should be the main concern of the leader to avoid routes that require the use of a rope and, if there is danger involved, a detour must be made. However, situations can sometimes occur that demand a change of route and a steep ascent or descent. You may need to descend quickly off a ridge to avoid a coming storm or to surmount a ridge to avoid difficult bog and marshland. On such terrain a rope may be required for a variety of reasons. A particularly nervous person may only be able to move confidently on a steep slope if secured by a safety rope. If a member has suffered a minor knee or ankle injury, a safety rope can give the support required to surmount a steep incline. A fixed rope acting as a handline can similarly help when descending a moderate slope. In a more serious situation a rope can be used to give an injured person assistance and even extract a party from an exposed or difficult predicament. There is therefore a need for the leader to possess suitable rope techniques that can be followed by the non-climber. These techniques are not necessarily the same as those adopted by rock climbers and the leader of the walking party will rely on the use of the rope alone. It is recommended by the Mountain Leader Training Board that his experience should include the ability to lead both ascents and descents on easy ungraded rock; be able to select a safe route up a rocky hillside and know when to use the safety rope; be able to identify suitable belay anchors and use them effectively and quickly; be able to abseil using the classic method; be able to hold a falling second man and to know the standard signals and calls for communication. He should also be able to give basic instruction in these items and correct common faults.

The only equipment that the leader requires is a nylon rope. Take note that a thin rope will make for difficulty in holding and will also cut into the skin. A nylon rope will last a long time if properly looked after, will not absorb water, is strong and has a great capacity to absorb shock. However, it has a comparatively low melting point so one rope should never be permitted to run across another rope. The type of rope most suited for carrying on a trek is the 9-mm ($\frac{3}{8}$-in) diameter 120-ft (36-m) or 45-metre (145-ft) nylon rope. Such a rope can be used to give assistance on steep ground, assist in crossing swollen streams or rivers and, in the event of a casualty, can be used in the construction of a Piggott rope stretcher (Fig. 102). The construction of the two main types of climbing ropes, the hawser and the kernmantal, is shown in Fig. 69.

Care of the Rope

The rope carried by a walking party may rarely be used, nevertheless it is essential that it is carefully looked after so that if required in an emergency it will stand up to the strain imposed, as in an abseil, when the rope is required to support the full weight of a person. At the extreme it must be able to stand the shock of a heavy fall. Take care of the rope and, when wet, dry it by spreading the rope in loose loops in an airy place. Never store it wet or in a damp unventilated room, nor store the rope in a hot place

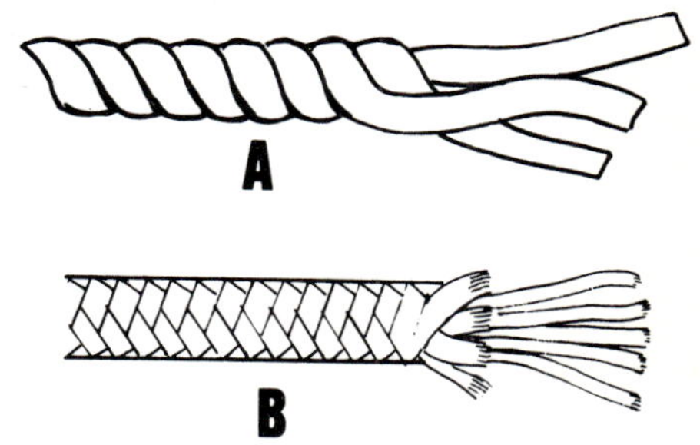

FIG. 69 Types of rope: A – hawser-laid, where three strands are twisted together to form a rope; B – kernmantal rope has a central core of nylon filament and a covering of braided coloured nylon sheath.

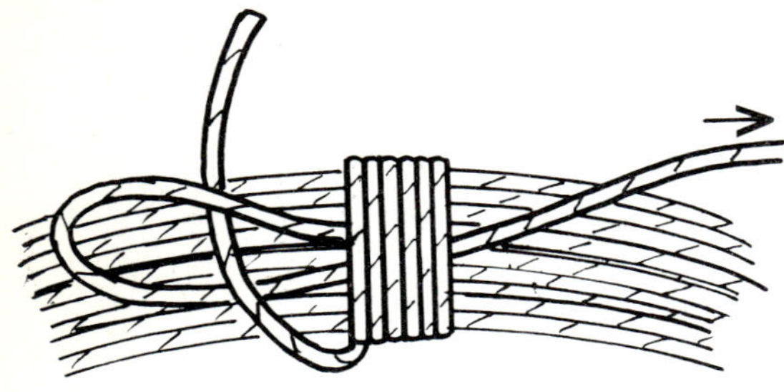

FIG. 70 Whipping the ends of coiled rope (see text). Do not make more than six turns in case the rope is needed quickly.

or dry it near a fire as this will cause the rope to go tight and stiff. Storing it exposed to strong sunlight can have the same effect. Make sure that if the rope is used frequently it is checked regularly for wear and damage. The rope should be checked by an expert and the strands of hawser rope examined inside for wear due to grit getting into the rope. Slight burring of the fibres on the outside of the rope will not weaken the rope much but wear inside the rope is dangerous and a warning of weakness and age. If a rope has suffered a severe shock or overstrain by taking a heavy fall it must never be used for climbing or abseiling.

You can coil the rope in the hands or over the knee and foot. It is necessary to avoid putting a twist in each turn by coiling the rope in a figure of eight with a half turn to the left and a half turn to the right each time round. If the rope is supple these twists can be shaken out for carrying and will, in any case, cancel each other as the rope is drawn for use. When the rope is coiled whip the ends by making a small loop with the one end of the rope, then make at least three turns with the loose end around the coiled rope and loop (Fig. 70). Now run the loose end through the loop and pull the loop tight. The rope can be carried over the shoulder or with the coils equally divided like the two shoulder straps of a pack.

Ascending and Descending Slopes

The safe ascent up a steep slope using a rope involves several techniques. At all times the person on the rope (the second man) must be safeguarded against the possibility of a fall and injury by the leader who holds and controls the rope. The leader must also be secured in case of the second man falling and pulling him from his secure point. The rope is therefore initially tied (belayed) to a secure point on the mountain and the leader and the second man must be tied onto the rope. The leader takes up any slack in the rope to the second man and then carefully supervises the second man's ascent to his position. Bringing up the second man therefore requires the techniques of the selection of a suitable belay point, securing the rope onto the belay point, tying onto the rope plus the safe management of the rope by the leader on the actual ascent. We will look first at suitable knots.

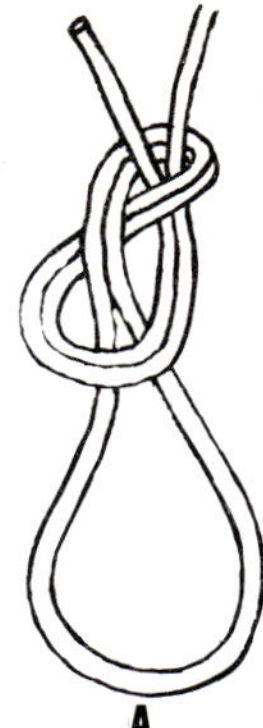

FIG. 71 The figure-of-eight knot: A – forming the knot; B – the knot complete with the end tied off with a thumb knot to make sure the knot cannot loosen.

KNOTS

The Figure-of-eight Knot

The figure-of-eight knot is the most basic knot used in climbing (Fig. 71A and B). It is easiest to tie and even if tied wrongly will result in an overhand knot which is still a safe knot. Other advantages are that it is stronger than a bowline knot which is the classic knot for tying yourself to the rope. It can be employed in a variety of ways and can be used when belaying to loop over rock-face spikes and flakes. It can even be used by two rock climbers as the sole knot employed through the whole operation of climbing a rock face. If there are more than two people on a rope the middlemen will use this knot to tie onto the rope. The figure-of-eight should be practised several times before tying a knot with a loop large enough to fit around the waist. Adjust the loop to fit by feeding one strand of rope through the knot, then tighten the knot and tie off the tail with a thumb knot to make sure that the knot cannot loosen (Fig. 71B).

The Overhand Knot

The overhand knot (Fig. 72) is a very simple, safe knot but after it has been tightened under load it is not so easy to untie as the figure-of-eight. If it is used as a waist-tie make the bight long enough to just fit over the shoulders, slip it down to the waist and then tighten by working the knot along. The overhand knot can be used to secure the end of any

FIG. 72 The overhand knot.

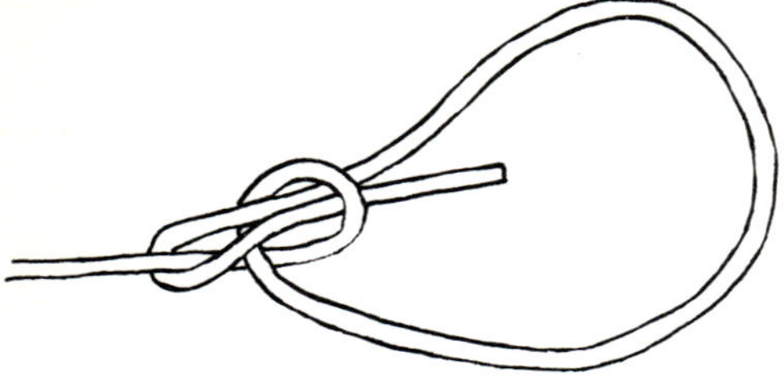

FIG. 73 The bowline. The end should be secured with two half-hitches or an overhand knot.

knot that may work loose and also in the construction of the Piggott rope stretcher (Fig. 102).

The Bowline Knot

The bowline is the standard end-man's knot tied around the waist (Fig. 73). It is a weaker knot than the figure-of-eight and not as simple but it is easier to adjust once around the body. It is helpful when tying the knot to remember that 'the rabbit (the end of the rope) comes out of the hole, around the tree, and back in again'. The knot should be secured with two half-hitches or an overhand knot. Take note that the bowline knot tied in a kernmantal rope is not always effective and must be tied off with a thumb knot or two half-hitches.

BELAY POINTS AND BELAYS

A belay point can be called upon to withstand considerable strain and therefore it is vital that the point selected is not likely to break away if a severe load is imposed upon it. It is also important to select a suitable point that is in line

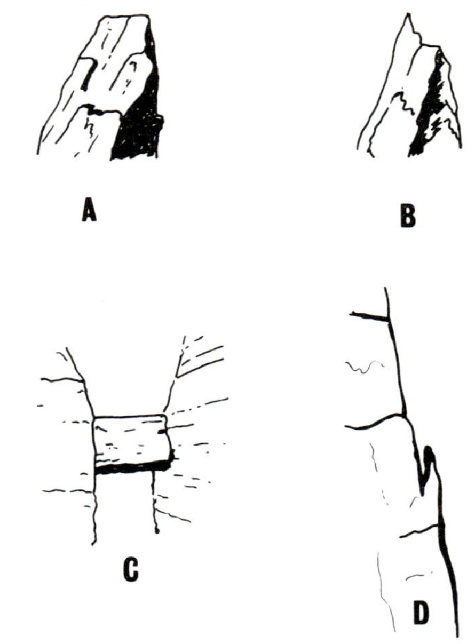

FIG. 74 Belay points: A and B – spikes; C – chockstone; D – flake.

with the expected direction of pull on the rope and, if possible, this point should be above waist level. Normally, on easy climbs belay points are not difficult to find. You have a choice of spikes, flakes or chockstones (Fig. 74). On the other hand a solid, firm tree-trunk growing out from the rock is also an ideal anchor. Test belay flakes and spikes by hitting them hard with the flat of the hand and once the rope is attached tug hard to make quite sure they cannot come away. Test chockstones by trying to prise them loose. Similarly make completely sure that a tree-trunk is as firm as it looks.

Spike Belay (Figure-of-eight)

The figure-of-eight spike belay is the simplest of all (Fig. 75). A figure-of-eight loop is tied at the end of the rope and dropped over a rock spike. An overhand knot could also be used. Take note that in all forms of belaying it is important that the leader is tied to the rope in a position where the second man is clearly visible. The belay loop should come down tight from above the waist with no slack, so as to keep him firm in the event of the second man falling or sudden tension on the rope. This tightness also keeps the rope securely in place on the anchor point. The figure-of-eight spike belay has the advantage over that form of spike belay tied off at the waist (see below) in that if the second man should require close assistance, the leader can untie himself from the rope and climb down to give help, leaving the second man supported directly from the belay point.

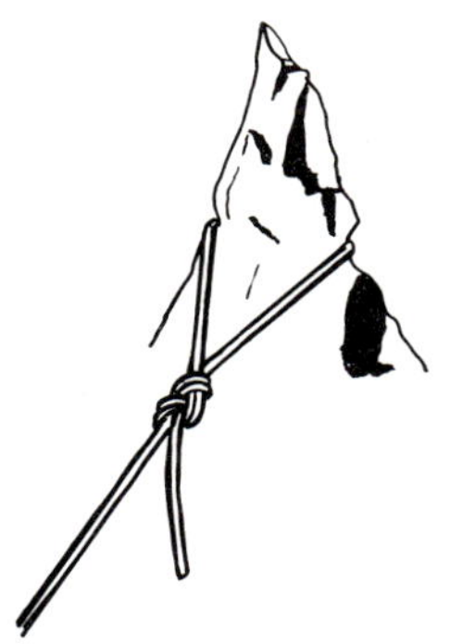

FIG. 75 Figure-of-eight belay tied on a rock spike.

Spike Belay (Tied off at Waist)

The rope is first tied around the waist with a bowline then run around the spike. The leader takes up his position so that no slack exists on the rope. A tuck of the free rope is taken through the waist loop to about an arm length then tied as a figure-of-eight or two or three half-hitches around the waist loop and both belay ropes that run from the rock (Fig. 76). It is recommended that the active rope is also included in the tie off and is shown as the dotted rope in Fig. 76. To gauge the right amount of rope

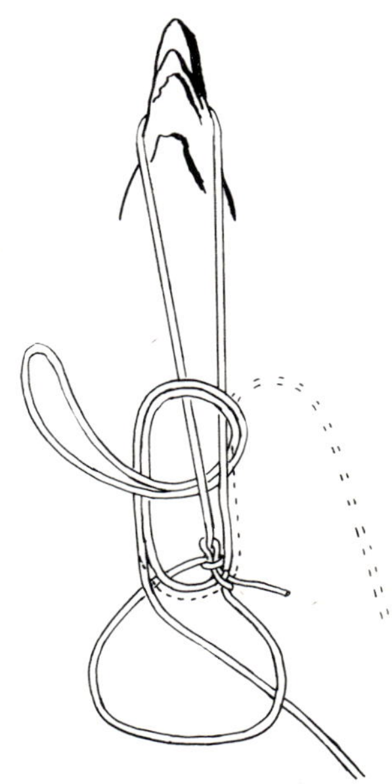

FIG. 76 Spike belay tied off at the waist (see text). The dotted rope shows how the active rope can be included in the tie-off.

between the waistline, around the spike, and back to the waistline needs practice. The disadvantage with the spike belay tied off at the waist is that you cannot untie the rope from your waist, should you need to climb down and give close assistance to the second man, without first untying the belay.

Thread Belay

The thread belay is the safest type of belay because it should resist a pull from any direction. Thread belays can be applied in various places such as where a large chockstone has jammed firmly in a crack with the crack narrower at the edge so that the chockstone cannot be pulled out, where two masses of rock join, or through a hole formed naturally in solid rock. Take a length of rope running from the knot on the waistline, double the rope and pass the bight around the chockstone or through the hole in the rock and back to the waist loop (Fig. 77). A tuck is now taken through the waist loop together with a tuck of rope of equal length from the active (dangling) rope. The four strands of rope (two loops) are tied off by taking both loops together back under the four ropes from the waist, then up and over to pull through the loop formed; now tighten the knot. The thread belay can also be used to belay onto a tree. The disadvantage of this method is that it uses a lot of rope and the double knot is bulky. The independent tie method where each rope is tied off separately onto the waist loop is slightly complicated but can also be used.

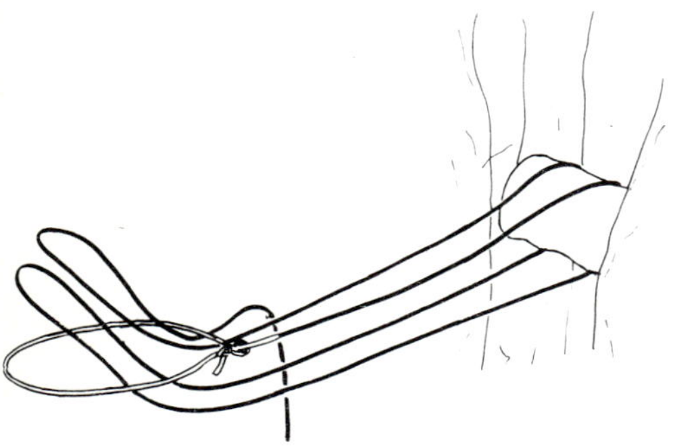

FIG. 77 The thread belay (for method of tying see text above).

BRINGING UP THE SECOND MAN

When controlling an ascent or descent the leader, who is belayed to a secure point, takes up a position in line with the rope leading from the anchor point to the climber (Fig. 78). The leader's sleeves are rolled down to protect his arms from the friction of the rope and, if possible, gloves should also be worn. The active rope is held, for the purpose of this description, in the leader's right hand (the directing hand). The right leg is advanced in line with the rope. The rope then runs around the back of the belayed leader above the waist loop to form the inactive rope which turns around the left forearm (the controlling arm), then is gripped by the left hand. Any slack in the rope from the belay point to the leader is taken up. The rope is now taken in until contact is made with the second man and then piled loosely at the leader's feet. The active rope, which is the rope that runs down to the climber, must always be taken in (or paid out) with the hand nearest to the climber. The ascent of the climber is controlled in the following way. When the rope is taken in, i.e. the slack is taken up as the climber ascends, the rope is passed from the right to the left hand by the right hand holding both ropes (Fig. 79A) while the left hand slides back

FIG. 78 Bringing up the second man showing the position of the belayed leader. Any slack in the rope to the belay point is taken up. The active rope is held in the leader's right hand and runs around his back to form the inactive rope which turns around his left forearm and is gripped by the left hand. The dotted line shows the position of the waist loop. It is vital that both ropes are not allowed to run across one another and generate friction, therefore clothing must cover the waist loop. Gloves should be worn.

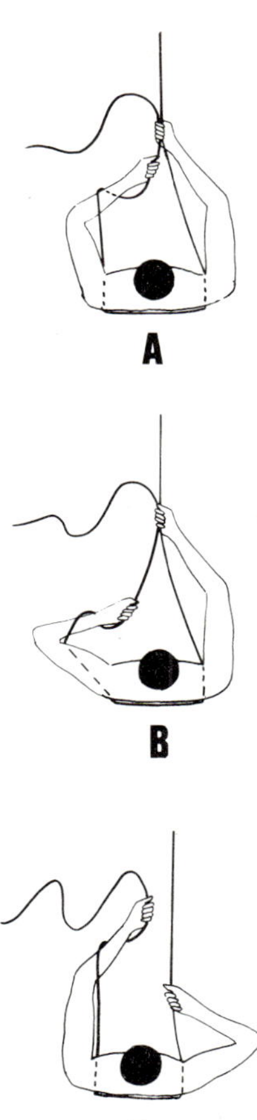

FIG. 79 Bringing up the second man – use of the hands and arms. The right hand controls the active rope and gloves are worn: A – the right hand holds both ropes while the left hand slides back – B; both hands grip their own ropes then the rope is taken in by the extension of the left arm and the flexion of the right – C. The right hand then slides forward to grip both ropes as in A and the action is repeated.

(Fig. 79B). Now the right and left hand grip their own ropes and the rope is then pulled around the waist by the extension of the left arm and the flexion of the right arm (Fig. 79C). The right hand then slides forward to the original position to grip both ropes. At no time are the hands removed from the rope.

It is important to note that the person ascending the slope does not attempt to climb up the rope, nor should he be physically pulled up the ascent. He must be encouraged by the leader to use hand- and footholds but the leader will take in the slack so that should the climber fall he can immediately be held and not tumble any distance. As the leader has taken up the slack in the rope from the belay point to himself and is also in direct line with the climber, if the climber slips the leader cannot be pulled off his point of support nor to one side. The calls used to control the ascent are given on page 112.

Paying out the Rope
Should it be necessary for the rope to be used to give protection during a descent when perhaps it is necessary to move off a difficult area or to lower an experienced member of the group to give assistance to another, the rope will be payed out by the belayed leader (the rope being held as described above). When the rope is payed out the two ropes are gripped in the controlling hand (in this case the left) and the directing hand (the right hand) is drawn back and grips the rope. The controlling hand releases the rope and the directing hand is extended forward to pay out the active rope before both ropes are gripped by the controlling hand again and the action is repeated. At no time are the hands removed from the rope.

Holding a Falling Second Man
The leader, belayed to a secure point, must at all times be alert and ready should the second man fall. With the moderate type of terrain envisaged for hill walks and the close supervision exercised over the second man the question of anyone being exposed to great danger and falling some distance should not arise. Nevertheless, should the second man slip only a few feet, the leader must be ready to take the strain with both hands in front of the stomach and the elbows tucked in. The legs are braced, particularly so the leg on the side of the active rope, and the body leans forward on the belay which is now pulled very tight at the waistline. In the event of a heavy fall the leader will let the rope run at first but gradually checks the fall with the friction of the rope around his body.

Use of the Triple Bowline
A nervous person in an intimidating situation will welcome a stable rope attachment. The triple bowline is recommended by the Mountain Rescue Committee as the best knot to use for lowering or raising a person and is tied

on the doubled end of the rope (Fig. 80). The three loops are adjusted for one to pass around the waist and the other two around each thigh. The knot effects a really secure harness. The triple bowline can be adjusted so that one loop runs across the chest and over the shoulder and two are run around the thighs. The triple bowline can also be used to raise or lower an injured person. The triple bowline can be difficult to adjust but a perfect fit can be obtained by using the end of the rope doubled to match the second's height and the bowline then tied with the doubled rope around the thigh. The loops formed should fit the person.

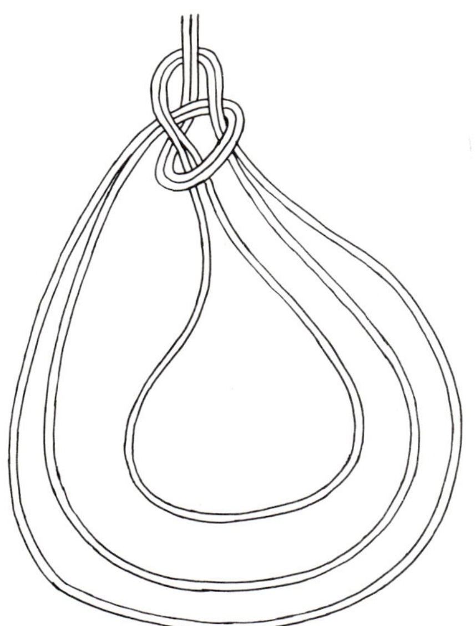

FIG. 80 The triple bowline. The centre loop becomes the long shoulder loop and the two outside loops are adjusted to thigh size.

ABSEILING

Abseiling is the technique that enables a climber to quickly descend to a lower level after completing a climb, perhaps to retire from too difficult a pitch or to move off an exposed ridge because of inclement weather. The leader of a hill walk would utilize this technique to quickly lower himself to render assistance to an injured person. Abseiling relies on the friction of the rope on the body. It is not a technique that is based on strength, nor does it require great skill. The anchor point for the abseil rope must be absolutely firm with no chance of the rope slipping off. If the anchor point is sharp protect the rope with an anorak, sweater or rucksack so that it cannot be frayed. A high belay point is best as it enables the climber to commence the abseil from a comfortable stance. The rope used should be 9-mm ($\frac{3}{8}$-in) nylon doubled with a figure-of-eight knot in the middle which will go over the abseil point. The classic method of abseil is simple and safe and is the most suited for the leader of a hill-walking party to employ (Fig. 81). It involves the following technique. After belaying the rope securely, throw the two ends of the rope down the descent so that they both reach the point to which you wish to descend. The rope must not be twisted. The climber stands astride the rope facing the anchor point so that the doubled rope is held in the left hand and passes between his legs. The rope is

FIG. 81 The classic method of abseil on steep ground using a single doubled rope. Whenever possible use a safety rope tied around the waist.

now taken behind and around the right thigh, up across the chest and over the left shoulder, front to rear, then across the back so that the hanging rope is held in the right hand. If you are left handed the position of the rope will be opposite and so will the use of the hands. The climber now moves over the edge carefully so as not to disturb the anchored rope nor let it slip from the upper thigh to behind the knee or off the shoulder. If the ground is vertical the climber should walk backwards down the rock, keeping his legs and body fairly straight with his feet level and about 18 ins (50 cm) apart.

The position of the rope, held in the right hand, controls the speed of the descent. The lower hand takes the strain and the upper hand steadies the body on the rope. If the right hand is brought around to the front the friction on the rope is increased and the rate of descent decreases; if the rope is wet or there is a long length of rope hanging below, the rope may not slide easily over the shoulder and it will be necessary to ease the rope by lifting it with the right hand. When abseiling down less steep ground the climber should turn sideways so that he can observe the terrain below more easily (Fig. 82). With either method the

FIG. 82 The classic method of abseil on less severe ground enabling the climber to look down. A safety rope should be attached to the waist whenever possible.

descent should be at a steady, smooth, walking pace and not include any leaps or bounds since this may place an unnecessary strain on the belay point. Where it is necessary to retrieve the rope to make a further descent the rope would not be tied to the belay point but doubled, then looped over it so that when the abseil is complete the rope can be pulled down. In this instance the anchor point must be smooth to permit the rope to be pulled down and not jam. Take note when practising that a safety rope must always be tied to the climber's waist to give maximum protection but the belayed climber covering the person descending should use a separate anchor point and not rely on the same point as the abseil rope. The leader should also be familiar with the technique of using half the rope as a safety rope and employing an independent belay. In this respect the 45-m (145-ft) rope, being longer, has a decided advantage over the 120-ft (36-m) rope. The two belay points selected must be close together and the length of rope used as a safety rope give cover to the bottom of the pitch.

FIXED ROPES

A fixed rope can be used in a descent to assist the nervous members of the party. The rope should be tied with numerous overhand knots to form wrist loops then secured firmly at the top and bottom of the descent and at any other suitable point that will give additional security to the rope (Fig. 83). It should not be used in any situation where a slip could be dangerous. The fixed rope is therefore

FIG. 83 A well-secured fixed rope with wrist loops (overhand knots) tied can help those of nervous disposition when on a descent but it is not suitable for use where a slip could be dangerous, as in precipitous country.

limited in use. Only those with considerable experience of the mountains should walk in precipitous terrain, and in these conditions, it will be necessary when crossing exposed sections of a walk, to secure each individual separately. The fixed rope is not suitable for such situations.

PREPARATION AND TRAINING

Not all mountains and hill areas are of the same scale. In some areas the country is more rugged and lonely, the distance to civilization longer, the weather can be harsher. In such regions a party that is poorly prepared and led can soon be in difficulties for even a minor accident unless treated properly can develop into a more serious incident. The preparation of the group is most important and the technical competence of the leader needs to be sound.

A party that is to trek over steep terrain should be given pre-expedition training and have instruction that includes the basics of ropework and its application on steep ground. It can be far too late to await the occurrence of a serious incident and then, in a situation of stress and possibly bad weather, attempt to instruct group members in the use of rope techniques. However, pre-expedition training gives confidence, adds to safety and can be extremely interesting and enjoyable. Training can comprise formal rope instruction perhaps on a local outcrop of rock, or it can be integrated as part of a walk. During a training walk the party may be routed via an outcrop of rock and instruction given in rock scrambling, rope management and communication. This form of practice can present a welcome break in a long walk and make the venture more interesting and purposeful. It also makes for group interest and alertness, and provides the education and training of potential leaders or assistant leaders.

Rock Scrambling

Rock scrambling is a means of learning the elementary skills of climbing. The facilities and equipment required are simple. Near many towns or villages boulders and rocks can be found, perhaps in a wood, field or on a heath and are often located on soft grass or on sandy or peaty soil. Provided such outcrops consist of good firm and not loose or flaky rock, these can offer a good facility for rock scrambling. A pair of thin-soled pumps that are snug fitting and laced tight, or Vibram-soled boots, can be worn. Laces must not dangle. Slacks should be loose fitting to allow the knees to bend easily, so tight-fitting jeans are unsuitable. A strong belt gives good support to the waist. A loose, warm sweater worn over a shirt will allow free arm movement and should be tucked into the belt. Finger and toe nails need to be cut short. The leader should select suitable boulders no higher than twice a person's height. The basic techniques listed below should be taught and the scrambling supervised closely. Ideally, the ratio of instructors to pupils should be 1:2. Take note that a single outcrop can offer a variety of climbs (Fig. 84). The length of the climbs and the degree of difficulty can often be increased by including a girdle traverse. It is therefore possible to make completely different climbing moves on one outcrop and yet be near the ground all the time. It must be stressed that routes selected should be within the capabilities of students and emphasis placed on moving from one safe position to another. This form of training will give valuable confidence and if time permits and the party are interested, can be developed at a later stage into more challenging climbs on larger boulders with the cover of a top rope. As a guide, if the boulder is three times as high as the climber, the support of a second climber and a top rope is needed. The following points are important when rock scrambling.

FIG. 84 Rock scrambling. A large boulder of firm rock located on soft grass or sandy soil can provide the beginner with a variety of good basic climbs

Basic Technique

(a) Look carefully at the rock for footholds and handholds. Work them out in advance before you start to climb.
(b) Watch where you place your feet and keep your heels down.
(c) Stand upright away from the rock and with handholds low.
(d) Maintain three points of contact and only move one limb at a time.
(e) Test each hold and beware of loose rock.
(f) If you feel insecure carefully retrace your step and handholds.

Group Scrambling

(a) Follow the leader's route carefully.
(b) Don't crowd each other on the rock.
(c) If a stone is dislodged shout 'below' as loudly as possible to warn others.

Communication

Climbers must have clear communication and a distinct mutual understanding to ensure they are always well protected by their fellow climber(s) when moving on exposed rock faces. It is important that the leader of a walking expedition planning to cross steep ground instils this standard of understanding among his group. The calls to be made in bringing up the second man by the belayed leader and second man are based on recognized rock climbing calls and are as shown in the table below.

The purpose of training a group in these elementary climbing techniques is obviously to safeguard the group if they have to cross difficult, steep ground but it can also awaken young people to the additional challenge and adventure that is ever present in the hills and mountains. Those who, from their introduction to rope work and rock scrambling, find they are attracted to rock climbing should be advised how and where they can obtain further instruction in actual climbing techniques. Group training in rock scrambling and rope work will also

Call	*By*	*Action*
TAKING IN	Leader	The belayed leader pulls up the slack in the rope attached to the second man.
THAT'S ME	Second man	The second man acknowledges as the rope tugs at his waist. The leader puts on gloves.
CLIMB WHEN YOU'RE READY	Leader	The leader is ready to bring up the second man, the rope is around his back and gripped in two hands. The second man prepares to climb.
CLIMBING	Second man	The second man commences to climb.
AYE-AYE	Leader	The leader acknowledges the second man's call and takes in the rope.
TAKE IN	Second man	The second man indicates to the leader that he wants the slack rope taken in. The leader takes in.
SLACK	Second man	The second man indicates that the rope is too tight. The leader pays out some rope.
HOLD	Second man	The second man indicates that he is about to fall. The leader immediately braces himself.
TIGHT ROPE	Second man	The second man indicates that he wants assistance from the rope. The leader takes in all the slack then pulls on the active rope according to the circumstances.

assist the leader to appreciate more fully the ability of his party and to relate this ability to the planning of suitable expeditions. It is extremely important that he can appreciate the limits of what can be attempted by a group who have no rock-climbing experience. The training will also enable the leader to advise his group on mountain safety, how to recognize potentially dangerous terrain and the divide between rock climbing and rock scrambling. The training outlined above is a safeguard and it is stressed that it is the first duty of the leader of novice walking parties to avoid areas that necessitate the use of the rope.

Rivers and Mountain Streams

Streams and rivers are an integral part of the mountain environment and an appreciation of the difficulties they can present, particularly so when in spate, and the techniques needed to cross them in an emergency situation is important for the walker. It must be stressed that crossing rivers or mountain streams when in spate is an emergency procedure which should only be attempted when the water is fordable and a rope can be used to safeguard the group as they cross; also that the alternatives to taking such action should present a greater element of danger than the operation of crossing the water. However, in normal conditions small mountain streams are not difficult to ford. When crossing a mountain burn try to keep the feet dry but do not attempt to cross by jumping from boulder to boulder. Vibram-type soles will slip on greasy rock and nailed boots will do likewise if the rock is very smooth; the result can be a heavy fall. It is far wiser, in such circumstances, to remove your socks and wade the burn in boots worn on bare feet, then quickly dry your feet on the other side and replace your socks. Fast-moving water can be a powerful and at times a dangerous force. It is extremely difficult to wade safely in fast water that is above waist level and therefore the crossing of deep rivers and also streams that are in flood should be avoided. It is far safer to make a detour to a bridge or an easily fordable part. If this is not possible the leader must consider setting up camp and waiting for the water level to subside. Should an emergency situation arise where the circumstances dictate that the water must be crossed, the greatest care must be taken to reduce risk to the group. The following paragraphs aim to assist the potential leader to understand the characteristics of mountain streams and rivers so that he can appreciate the features of fast water.

The characteristics of streams and rivers are the same the world over. Mountain rivers and streams normally flow rapidly near their source then gradually slow down as they reach lower land. Where a river (or stream) runs straight and the banks are of even height the main current and deepest part is normally in the centre (Fig. 85). Where the river runs straight but one bank is higher than the other, the faster current and the deepest part are usually close to the high bank (Fig. 86). If there is a bend, the current will take the outside of the bend and this will be the deepest part (Fig. 87). On a bend the outside bank can be undercut by the action of the water, making the bank dangerous to stand on. The bed of a mountain stream or river is rarely even and there will be deep and shallow spots though the bottom is often smoother between rapids. The water is usually shallower and the flow slower where the waterway widens. If the river or stream spreads and splits into several channels the level may drop and the pressure of water will be reduced well above the channels. Such an area can be the safest place to cross. When selecting a point to cross make sure that there are no obstructions such as trees, partially submerged branches or barbed wire that could snag either the rope or a person. Strong currents and eddies should be avoided. High banks can make entry and exit from the river very difficult but a flat shingle or pebble shore often leads out into gradually deepening water. It is extremely important that the leader carries out a very thorough recce of the area and is satisfied that he has found the best place possible to ford the river before any attempt is made to cross. His recce may take time and he should look both upstream as well as downstream. As there may be a considerable variation in the depth and speed of water in even a mile, it is best to recce the upstream area thoroughly. On the other hand, a mountain burn running into a lake will slow down nearer the entry to the lake for the ground is normally flatter. The water may be deeper at this point but the current steady. It must be stressed that no attempt should be made to test the force of the water without being secured to the bank. A light or small person

FIGS 85-87 Cross-sections through rivers.

FIG. 85 Where a river runs straight and the banks are of even height, the faster current and deepest part will normally be in the middle.

FIG. 86 Where the river runs straight and one bank is higher than the other, the faster current and deepest water will normally be close to the higher bank.

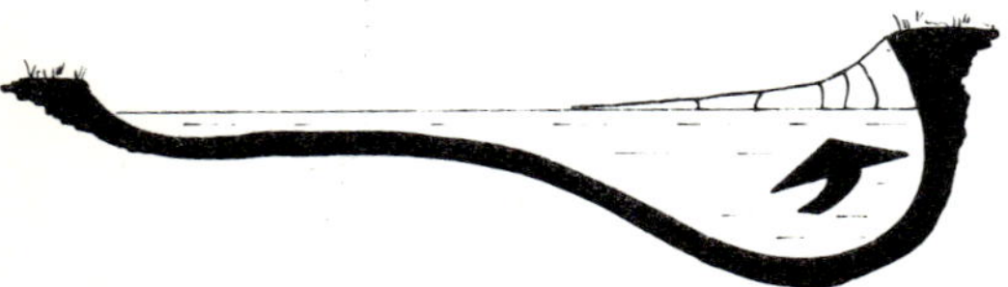

FIG. 87 Where a bend occurs, the faster current and deepest part will be on the outside of the bend.

could be swept off his feet in a strong current well before a tall heavier person, and the leader will need to take this fact into consideration both when testing the force of the water and also in the actual crossing.

Before a crossing the leader should check that each individual has prepared himself and his gear and has been fully briefed as to the plan to be carried out. As previously noted, boots should be worn when fording to protect the feet but socks should be taken off and put on dry on the other side. Trousers are also best taken off to reduce water friction and then put on dry when the river has been crossed. When carrying a pack ensure that the pack can be released quickly if needs be, so undo the waist belt and loosen the shoulder straps. Also take off any bulky clothing that could hinder the quick release of the pack. The pack should be made as buoyant as possible by placing empty mess tins, plastic containers, polythene bottles, and sealed polythene bags, etc. in the sack. The leader should, if necessary, recap on the type of knots to be used to tie on to the rope then supervise the tying or allocate the task to a competent deputy leader.

CROSSING WITHOUT A ROPE

Only in a dire emergency, such as going for help after a serious accident, should an attempt be made to cross deep or fast water without the help of a safety rope. If only one person is involved then he should first recce the bank to find the safest possible point to cross, bearing in mind the characteristics of rivers and their flow as noted previously. When fording a river or fast-flowing stream a stout stick will serve as a useful third 'leg'. Face upstream, so that the force of water cannot press against the backs of the legs and cause the knees to give, and use the stick to probe for a depth and to act as a support on the upstream side. When three or more persons are involved in a crossing the following techniques can be applied but the greatest care is still needed:

Method (a)

The party should cross in a crocodile of three or more persons (Fig. 88). They

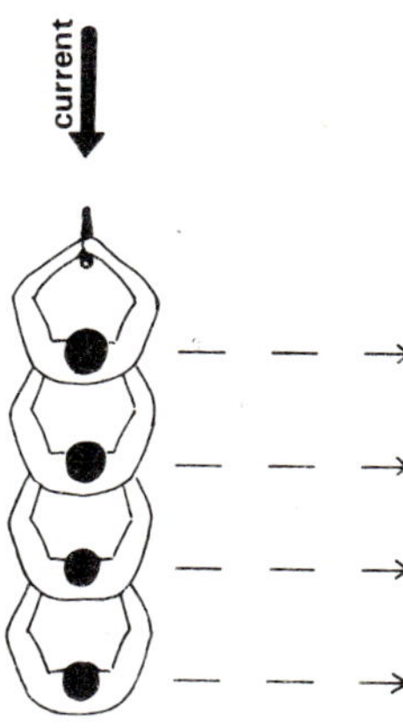

FIG. 88 Crossing a river without a rope, in crocodile formation (see text).

face into the flow of the current, which is not necessarily the actual direction of the river, for the current may run at an angle to the river bank. The heaviest person is positioned second in line from the front and the front man can make use of a stout stick, as described above. Each member on the crocodile holds firmly onto the person in front. On a given signal from the front man the party take shuffle steps sideways in unison. The advantage of this technique is that only one person, the front man, is exposed to the direct force of the current and he has the support of the rest of the party.

Method (b)

The party can cross in groups of three (Fig. 89). Two persons face inwards and the third faces upstream. Heads are kept close together, arms are firmly linked and feet well apart. Only one person will move at a time so that two are always able to give support.

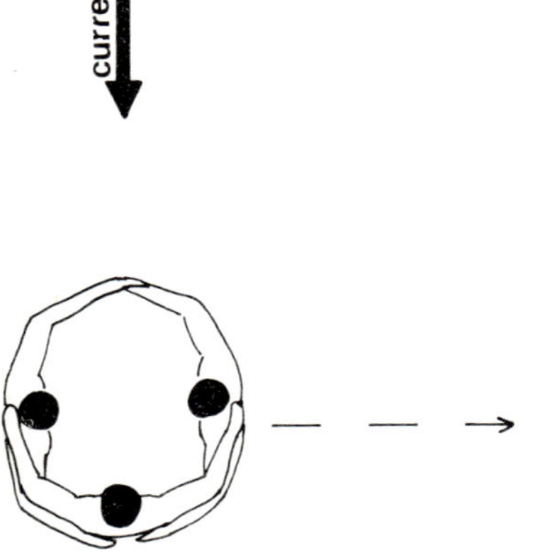

FIG. 89 Crossing a river without a rope, in groups of three (see text).

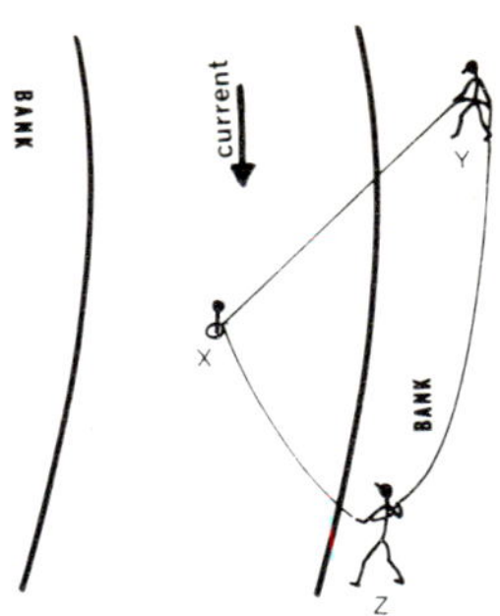

FIG. 90 Crossing a river using a rope moving from the right to the left bank. The leader, X, is tied onto the rope. Should X slip, Y will let the rope run while Z pulls X ashore but both supporters should be prepared to move downstream to keep X on the surface.

CROSSING USING A ROPE

The 120-ft (36-m), 9-mm ($\frac{3}{8}$-in.) safety rope can be used to attempt the safe crossing of a three-man (or bigger) party in the following way:

(a) The rope is tied to form a circle then the leader, or an experienced strong member of the party, X, ties a loop in the rope with a figure-of-eight knot and slips the loop over his shoulders. Party members Y and Z take up the rope (see Fig. 90) then X wades into the river where the current is slack. He faces upstream so that if the force of water increases it cannot press against the backs of his legs and

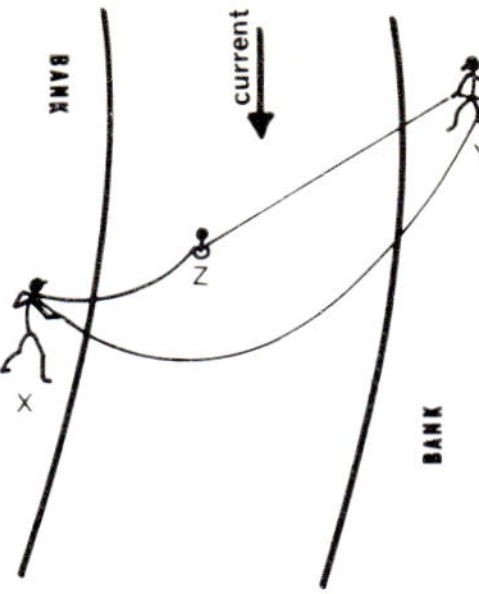

FIG. 91 When X has crossed he supports Z as he crosses but X is downstream of Y so that if Z slips, X will pull him ashore on his side. (Y will cross in a similar manner to X but supported by X and Z on the far bank.)

cause his knees to give. He takes small careful shuffle steps to keep in constant firm contact with the river bed. If his hips are angled so that the hip nearest the far bank is upstream of the other and kept at about 45° to the current, he can use the pressure of water against his body to help 'ferry glide', that is, push him towards the far bank even though his course may be partially downstream due to the pressure of the water. As he moves across Y and Z allow the rope to pass through their hands. Should X slip and be swept away, Y will let the rope run while Z pulls and guides him ashore. In such circumstances, should Y try to pull X to the side against the current X could be forced under by the pressure of the water. Both supporters, therefore, need to be prepared to move downstream and so keep him on the surface.

(b) When X has successfully crossed he leaves the waist loop tied in the rope. Z ties on his own loop and the routine is repeated with Y and X supporting the rope, but with X positioned downstream of Y so that should Z slip, he will be pulled ashore by X (Fig. 91).

(c) Y, the last man to cross, will cross in a similar manner to X, but this time helped by X with Z downstream acting as the rescuer to pull him to the side should he slip.

(d) If there are more than three people in the party, once two people have crossed to the far bank, one person will hold the rope on the original bank while two control the crossing on the far side, one of whom will be positioned upstream of the person crossing to give support on the rope, the other downstream to pull in the person should he fall or be swept off his feet.

Lightning

Lightning cannot be regarded as a common hazard in Britain, but each year fatalities do occur, though these are rarely among mountaineers or hill walkers. In some regions of the Alps lightning can be extremely dangerous. However, to encounter an electrical storm in the hills can be quite an alarming experience and the leader of a walk should be aware of danger areas and also safe zones that exist on both high and flat terrain.

Electrical storms usually give a clear visual and audible warning of their approach, by the nature of the sky and the noise of advancing thunder. The noise of thunder can be considerable but it should be borne in mind that it is quite harmless and results from the rapid expansion of air as it is heated by the passage of lightning. It is possible to roughly estimate the distance of lightning from where you are by counting the time between the flash and the sound of thunder. An interval of 5 seconds indicates that the lightning is about a mile away - sound travels at about 1100 feet per second and there are 5280 feet to the mile. When an electrical storm threatens, metal objects may buzz, hair can become raised, the skin may tingle, ice axes hum and spark and prominent local features glow in a bluish light.

When such indications predict an electrical storm it is very unwise to continue walks along ridges or peaks for lightning strikes tend to concentrate on projections such as these. It is also unwise, when on a plateau or on moorland, to shelter near large boulders or trees for they can attract a strike. The Mountain Leader Training Boards advocate that as a high point, such as a hill, is the prominent feature of an area and a possible strike point, there tends to be a

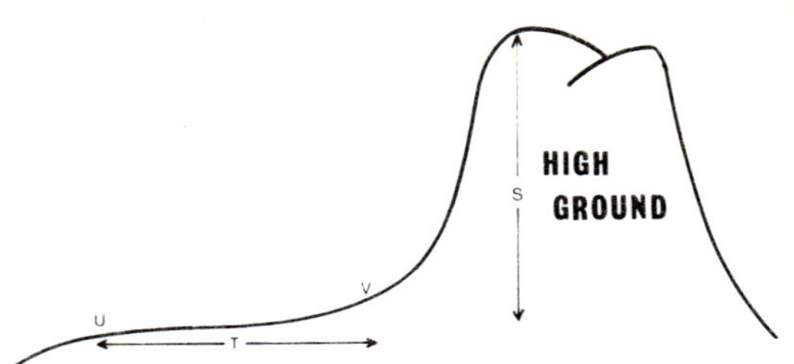

FIG. 92 During an electrical storm in hill country shelter in the safe zone of a hill as follows: the peak of the hill (S) must be at least 6 m (20 ft) high; the safe zone (T) will equal this distance horizontally; sit in the centre of the area U – V and keep away from the slope leading down to V.

relatively safe zone associated with the actual high point. To have such a safe zone the high point must be at least 6 m (20 ft) high to offer a relatively safe zone of the same distance out from the point. (Fig. 92). Avoid keeping close to a cliff or a steep surface below a peak as you could receive earth currents dissipated from a strike above. When on flat or gentle ground avoid taking shelter in a hole for if there is a nearby strike the charge will jump the gap caused by the hole, perhaps with fatal results for anything taking cover there. It is similarly unwise to shelter in small caves during an electrical storm. There may be a minor expansion of natural fissures that will conduct electrical earth charges. These can spark across the gap in the earth. Take note that a lightning strike will run down a crack in preference to solid rock and if the area is wet the danger is greater so avoid sheltering in rock fissures. Keep away from large boulders (Fig. 93) and walls, for a

FIG. 93 It is dangerous to sit or stand near boulders during an electric storm – you may attract the charge from a nearby strike as it runs to earth.

FIG. 94 In an electrical storm it is best to sit on your rucksack, tent or rope on a broken scree slope or dry bracken out in the open. Place your hands in your lap with your knees up.

human body sheltering close-in can attract the charge. Metal fences should be avoided as they are good conductors of electricity.

The safest course to take is to stay out in the open. Even though such storms can be accompanied by heavy rain, keeping dry should not be a problem if you are properly clad with waterproof and warm clothing. Find an area of bracken (the drier the better) or, if on a hill, a broken scree slope (Fig. 94), then sit on a dry rucksack, tent or rope with your hands in your lap and your knees up so as to keep the points of the body in contact with the ground as close as possible. By doing so you ensure that in the event of a local lightning strike any current running through the ground would not pass through a vital part of the body. Do not divest yourself of small metal objects such as the torch or compass. They are unlikely to attract lightning any more than the human body does and they can be vital to your safety.

It should be appreciated that to be struck by lightning is not always fatal, for a person can receive only part of a nearby ground strike which quickly dissipates like the fine roots of a large tree through the earth. It is possible to receive a shock by induction when standing near a point struck by lightning. Although such a strike may vary in power, it is the product of a very large current but lasts only thousandths of a second and often does not convey the same damage that could be produced by a lower current over a longer period.

To recap: when an electrical storm is indicated, act quickly, get off high ground and find a suitable position in the open or, if in hill country, a safe zone shaded by a high point, then sit the storm out as indicated above.

Snow and Ice

Although this book aims to cover the techniques and equipment required for walking hills and mountains in summer, it is necessary to fully appreciate the difficulties that can occur with a sudden change to winter-like conditions. At height the weather can alter quickly and what started as a pleasant walk up a well-defined path on a fine day can turn into something quite different, with high winds and a snow blizzard, obliterating the path completely. These extremes are not unknown in very early or late summer. Even in summer a walk over a high mountain ridge may take you across areas of snow or ice and care is needed. Take note that walks at height in early spring or late autumn should not be planned if valley temperatures are low, for freezing conditions will exist on the upper mountain slopes. If the temperature is low, rain, drizzle or intense low cloud at height can coat a path with treacherous ice and make the surface extremely slippery. In these conditions composition-soled boots will not grip and great care therefore needs to be taken. If snow has fallen, cornices, which are masses of overhanging snow, may be encountered on ridges, at the edge of an escarpment, or on the tops of gullies (Fig. 95). The line of fracture on a cornice is much further down the slope than many people realize. Therefore, if you have to traverse a ridge keep well down the slope to the windward side, completely away from the lip. Melting snow can avalanche, so avoid gullies and steep snow slopes. As you walk, snow will tend to ball under the soles of your boots and make walking unsteady and difficult so frequently kick or scrape off the snow. Where, under warmer conditions, streams run, they will now form sheets of ice beneath the snow and can, if the snow is shallow, require care when crossing. It must be stressed that if it is deliberately planned to cross frozen areas of ice and snow then crampons should be worn and ice axes carried. Each person should be instructed in the use of the ice axe, including the method of using it as a brake when a slip occurs, and also in the methods of safeguarding one another when on ice-bound surfaces.

In the event of being stranded at high level in snow conditions, protection must be obtained as soon as possible. A simple but effective way to obtain protection from the wind is to dig into a deep snow slope to make a cave which is well hollowed out but has a small entrance. The warmth generated by body

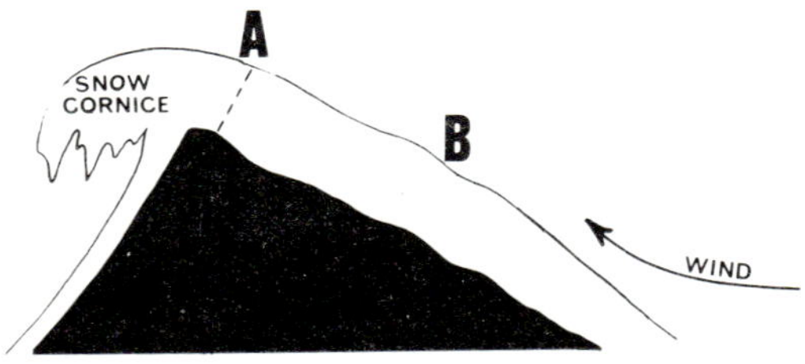

FIG. 95 The dangers of a snow cornice. The line of fracture at A is much further down the slope than is often appreciated. Keep well down the slope to the windward side. B is a safe point to contour the ridge.

heat in the comparatively small space will then help to keep the group warm. If on open ground, dig a hole about 2 ft (60 cm) deep and make a wall of snow on the windward side. Ground sheets should then be used to construct a lean-to bivouac shelter. If tents are carried scoop out an area to take the tent, then surround the tent on the windward side with a high snow wall.

The avoidance of danger should be paramount in the leader's mind and he should use all the resources available to him to ensure that his group are not exposed to any undue risk. The use of the rope to provide a safe handline across a rime-covered path near a moderate descent may need to be considered, or individuals may need to be tied on and the belayed leader help them up an ice-covered slope. However, if very difficult conditions are encountered, the leader should NEVER HESITATE TO TURN BACK. It must be appreciated that if a project is planned to cross areas of snow and ice then the preparation of the group in snow and ice techniques must be undertaken. Such a project should not be attempted with novices.

Exposure

Exposure can be defined as a severe chilling of the body's surface leading to a progressive fall in the inner core temperature to such an extent that the body cannot restore its normal temperature. Exposure can be a combination of cold, exhaustion, anxiety and mental stress. When mountain accidents are analysed it is rarely found that cold alone proves fatal. However, exhaustion is a very important factor for if the body's reserves of energy are depleted, the deep core temperature cannot be maintained and exposure is the result. It should be noted that young people often do not possess the same mental and physical reserves as adults and are thus more susceptible to exposure. It is therefore of paramount importance that this factor is always borne in mind when planning expeditions and the greatest attention should be given to ensure that those of less mature years are not severely over-taxed.

SYMPTOMS

The symptoms of exposure are not always easy to detect and therefore it is necessary for a leader to know his party and to watch for uncharacteristic behaviour that can give warning of exposure setting in. The following are the symptoms of exposure, but it should be noted that not all these symptoms may occur, nor may they occur in this order:

(a) complaints of feeling cold, tired or listless;

(b) physical and mental lethargy, including failure to respond to and understand questions and instructions;

(c) uncontrollable shivering;
(d) unexpected and unreasonable behaviour;
(e) slowing down, stumbling or repeated falling;
(f) slurring of the speech;
(g) sudden bursts of unexpected energy;
(h) resistance to any aid offered and violent language;
(i) abnormality or failure of vision (when this occurs the person's condition can be serious);
(j) light-headedness;
(k) muscle cramp;
(l) ashen pallor;
(m) occasional fainting.

CAUSES

The causes of exposure can be environmental or individual in origin or a combination of both. Factors such as local temperature, wind strength, energy intake, water intake, clothing, stress and injury are relevant. In cold conditions an injured person in a state of shock can easily become an exposure casualty unless immediate action is taken to assist him. This is due to the fact that he may not be able to maintain his core temperature and all available means need to be applied to keep him warm.

Lapse Rate and Wind Chill

It is normally much colder on high land than in valleys for the air temperature drops by about 2/3°C (3/5°F) in 1,000 ft (300 m) with some variation according to humidity. This temperature drop is known as the 'lapse rate'. The combined cooling of low air temperature and wind speed is known as the 'wind-chill' effect. It should be noted that the cooling effect of the wind is most pronounced in lower wind speeds so that in the range of 0-15 mph (0-24 km/h) even small increases in the wind speed bring about considerable cooling. A strong wind can produce conditions that are normally experienced with colder temperatures. The wind-chill effect of a strong breeze registered as Force 6 (about 28 mph (45 km/h)) in an air temperature of 10°C (50°F) is equivalent to a slight breeze of Force 1 (about 2 mph (3 km/h)) at -12°C (10°F). The great danger to life in cold, wet weather is the general lowering of the body temperature due to a combination of cold, wind and wet clothing. If clothing is wet from profuse sweating, rain or sleet, the effect upon the body due to the cooling effect of saturated clothing may be equivalent to a reduction of 6°C (11°F) in the air temperature. The overall protection of the body from the wind cannot be too strongly stressed. A waterproof anorak is therefore essential and also a cagoule and over-trousers (see pages 10 and 12). Remember that the heat loss from the head is extremely high so ensure that the head is well covered.

Energy

A mountain trek can demand the same

calorific expenditure as a labourer engaged in heavy manual work. To attempt to maintain such an energy output over several days requires a very fit person adequately trained for the project and a diet comprising sufficient energy-producing food. A 10-12 mile (16-19 km) mountain walk involving 2,500-3,000 ft (800-1000m) of climbing a day necessitates an attractive balanced diet producing 4,000-plus calories per day and should include a high-energy snack at mid-day. Training for expeditions should therefore be graded, commencing with easier projects that require a moderate intake of calories, then gradually progressing to more advanced schemes that demand a higher degree of fitness and a greater calorie intake. At all times energy reserves must be maintained by avoiding activity that is beyond the strength of the participants and by ensuring a regular intake of suitable food. It is most important that sufficient energy reserves are conserved in case severe conditions of cold and high wind are encountered and these reserves are needed to combat exhaustion that could lead to exposure.

Water

Water is needed to keep the body cool and working efficiently (see page 128). The more intense the activity the greater the need for water. Lack of sufficient water leads to dehydration which can have serious consequences. Each 1000 calories of energy expended in summer requires about 1½ pints (0.8 l) of water. Take note that the thirst sensation is not an accurate reflection of the body's water requirements and that the body needs water to work efficiently even though the sensation of thirst may be absent. It is therefore advisable when engaged on a long trek to drink past the point of thirst quenching. It is possible to go into water debt and replenish lost fluid at the end of the day but, if the trek is a long expedition, it is wiser to drink a little fairly frequently and so ensure that the needs of the body are met. When on a long expedition it is necessary to replace salt that has been lost through sweat and passed out in urine, otherwise muscle cramp can be experienced. Taking salt dissolved in water will help to offset dehydration that could lead to a loss of mental and physical powers and result in exhaustion.

Fitness

Progressive training designed to familiarize personnel with the hardship of the wilds and difficult conditions will help to build up a tolerance to arduous conditions and, to a certain degree, the factors that cause exposure. Familiarization training which has both mental and physical benefits can therefore prove invaluable when situations are encountered that subject individuals to stress and cold. It should be appreciated that apprehension and a spirit of fear brought about by adverse conditions and perhaps lack of fitness can be transmitted from one person to another if not quickly checked. In such a situation, firm, cheerful, confident leadership is required with sensible actions made to combat difficulties and to steer the group to safety.

TREATMENT

Once a case of exposure is detected treatment must be immediate. It is *essential* that the victim is not allowed to exert himself further nor force himself on. Normally the core temperature of the trunk and brain remains constant at 98.4°F (37°C). The temperature of the skin, muscles and the extremities of the body are below this. The aim in treating exposure is to maintain the body's deep core temperature and return the overall temperature to normal. Should the core temperature fall, loss of muscular co-ordination and mental deterioration can occur, then unconsciousness, followed by heart and respiratory failure and finally death results. It is therefore critical that any treatment given does not increase the peripheral circulation for further heat loss must be avoided at all costs. The first task is to insulate the body with all means available. Immediately erect a tent. Remove the victim's wet clothes and dry him, then get him into a sleeping bag and insulate him well. Make certain that the areas under the shoulders, buttocks and feet are particularly well insulated from contact with the ground otherwise more body heat will be lost. The victim can be warmed by placing hot rocks or bottles of hot water (insulated to avoid burning him) between the inner and the outer layers of his sleeping bag. The areas that are so important to heat are the vital organs – the heart, kidneys, liver, lungs and digestive system. If the number of heating units is limited place them in this order: the pit of the stomach, the small of the back, the armpits, the back of the neck and between the thighs. If such heating units are not immediately available put a fit person into the bag alongside the casualty to give him added body warmth. Light a stove in the tent and get as many people in as is possible to increase the air temperature in the tent but check that adequate ventilation is available all the time. If the victim can still take food, give him some provided it is in an easily digestible form. Hot drinks, such as hot milk with sugar added, are beneficial but do not force liquid on an unconscious person as he could be suffocated. Take note that alcohol should not be given nor should the skin be rubbed as the peripheral circulation will be increased and core heat lost. If respiration fails, give artificial respiration until the patient commences to breathe normally. However, the patient is not cured as soon as his body temperature returns to normal. The building up of his body heat and energy reserves by eating and resting will take time, so prolonged rest is essential.

Should the leader decide that it is better to remove the victim from the area rather than perhaps wait many hours before a rescue party can arrive, the way to improvise a stretcher is shown on page 137. But note that such an evacuation would only take place after all immediate field treatment had been applied and the leader satisfied that there was less risk to the casualty in attempting to evacuate him than in awaiting help. The stretcher crew who are to evacuate the casualty must continue to preserve the insulation of the patient during his journey to safety and so he must be well wrapped up, including his head and face. A polythene survival bag can help retain body warmth. Take care that the patient's mouth and nose are not covered so as to restrict breathing. The patient should be evacuated in the head-down position and a person who is not a stretcher bearer, should be detailed to check continually on the patient's condition to ensure that he does not vomit and choke, nor suffer respiratory or cardiac failure. Treatment at base should, if possible, be undertaken by a doctor. The recovery of a person in a warm environment can be spectacular but also misleading and he may, if not carefully nursed, suffer a relapse later. The rapid re-warming of the body by immersing the patient in a hot bath can be very effective. In severe cases of exposure the rapid re-warming of a victim by total immersion of the body in hot water at 113° F (45° C) can save life. If there is no bath thermometer available check that the water temperature is not too hot by immersing your elbow. The legs of the patient should be kept out of the water since it is necessary not to cause the dilation of the veins of the extremities and so reduce the blood volume. The temperature of the bath water will drop due to the cooling effect of the patient's body so replenish with hot water, continually checking the temperature. After about 15-20 minutes, or when the patient shows signs of perspiration, quickly remove him, in the prone position, to a very warm bed for a period of complete rest. This bath treatment does involve a degree of risk for the patient who is unconscious, the very young, the very old, or those of a frail disposition. The doctor may decide that the re-warming of the patient in a very warm room and bed with no pillow would be more appropriate treatment. The effects of the period of exposure are long term and require close care of the patient long after the initial and often dramatic improvement is recorded.

The subject of exposure is fairly complex and, as noted, involves a variety of factors but the steps necessary to avoid exposure are simple. Ensure that you have suitable warm clothing, avoid bad weather, have regular meals of energy-producing food, avoid very heavy loads and keep a steady comfortable pace over a reasonable distance per day.

Frostbite

Situations where extreme weather conditions could be encountered should always be avoided. However, high-level walkers in the early spring or late summer can encounter colder conditions and a forced bivouac with low temperatures may, in adverse circumstances, bring about the risk of frostbite. In the event of a casualty in such conditions the possibility of frostbite must be considered, for frostbite is closely associated with exposure. In an exposure case the body's surface is cooled with a reduction in the circulation made to maintain heat in the core. This reduced circulation greatly increases the possibility of frostbite.

SYMPTOMS

Frostbite is the partial or actual freezing of parts of the body such as the nose, cheeks, ears, hands and feet. As the skin freezes the blood vessels contract and constrict the flow of blood to the skin tissue so that the subcutaneous layers can be protected longer. In severe cases an outer layer of skin freezes followed by the subcutaneous tissues, muscle tissue and finally the bone freezes. Frostbite, whether it is confined to the skin surface or deeper, is a very serious condition. In acute cases the tissue becomes solid and immovable, the individual will become numb and drowsy, the eyesight fails and he loses consciousness. The initial stage is known as frostnip and is easily combated provided it is recognized in time. The symptoms of frostnip are a blanching (white appearance) of the skin and a cessation of feeling in the affected part, or a sensation of warmth following cold.

TREATMENT

Frostnip should be treated immediately and the affected part thawed out by bringing it into contact with warm parts of the body. Frostnipped fingers can be thawed out by being placed under the armpits; ears, by the warmth of hands that have been rubbed to generate additional warmth; feet should be placed against a companion's tummy.

Frostbite is prevented by providing the body with good insulation and keeping the face, ears, nose, wrists, hands and feet warm and dry. Circulation to the face can be improved through exercising the face muscles by wrinkling the nose and grimacing. Exposure to very cold conditions, especially in strong winds, should be limited; also avoid touching cold metal with bare hands.

Frostbite casualties should be evacuated to a place where expert medical help can be obtained. However, if the patient is immobilized by injury and the rescue party may take some time to reach the point, he should be immediately treated on the spot for exposure and shelter obtained, nourishment given and warmth applied. Do not attempt to re-warm the affected areas by exercise, rubbing with snow, applying direct heat as from a hot-water bottle or stove (though in the case of frostbite of the hands or feet warming of the arms or legs with hot-water bottles or hot stones suitably covered will help recovery of the afflicted part). Do not give alcohol nor touch or prick blisters. Treat frost-bite as you would a burn and apply a light sterile dressing after cleaning the area by dabbing with cotton wool and warm, soapy water, then cover it with warm material. It should be noted that once re-warming has taken place it is critical that the skin is protected from damage or re-cooling. No further use of the affected part should be allowed. However, the leader must appreciate that a person with a frozen foot is mobile, whereas after thawing has taken place he must be carried and the area is open to infection with the possibility of the injury re-freezing.

Treatment at base should be supervised by a doctor. Rapid re-warming by immersion in hot water that has a temperature of 42-43°C (108-109°F) is the recognized treatment. This method ensures that little time is lost and pain is not increased. In field conditions a Primus stove can be used to heat water in a container into which hands or feet can be immersed. Test the temperature of the water by using the elbow. Take note that a higher temperature will cause considerable discomfort and even severe pain to the victim so care is needed to ensure that the temperature is correct. If pain is experienced, give the patient pain-killing tablets, such as aspirin. Above all, avoid situations where there is the possibility of anyone suffering from frostnip or frostbite.

Heat Disorders

The effects of the sun and of heat on the human body can be quite serious. An understanding of the causes and treatment of heat disorders and of the methods to be employed to avoid such afflictions and illnesses is very necessary for those who will trek in hot conditions. Heat disorders can be caused by an inadequate water intake, loss of salt from the body, sunburn or inadequate time to acclimatize to hot conditions, or a combination of these factors. Once the body has been exposed to heat for several days it adapts to the increased temperature by recording a lower skin and core temperature, a reduction of salt in the urine and sweat, and a more efficient sweating mechanism. The body will also record a reduction in the heart rate when engaged in exercise and a higher overall tolerance to the warmer conditions. It should be noted that most heat disorders are due to water depletion rather than the actual effects of the sun.

WATER

It must be appreciated that the body cannot adapt to a low intake of water but the minimum required for life will vary in accordance with the degree of heat the body is subjected to and to the physical work undertaken. Approximately 5 pints ($2\frac{1}{2}$ l) is the average daily water requirement for the body. In addition for every 1,000 calories of expended energy in hot weather about $1\frac{1}{2}$ pints (0.8 l) of water is required. This increased intake of water is necessary to cool the surface of the body by evaporation and is given off in sweat. In very hot conditions the water requirement can increase to about 14 pints (7.8 l) per day. A good rule to employ in hot conditions is to drink 10 pints (5.6 l) of water per day plus 1 pint (0.5 l) for every hour of activity. As previously stated, the thirst sensation is not an accurate reflection of the body's water requirement and it is advisable when engaged in hard physical activity to drink past the point of thirst quenching. It should be noted that if the urine is scanty and highly coloured, more water should be drunk.

SALT

Prolonged exercise in hot weather such as trekking with a pack can lead to excessive sweating and a considerable loss of vital salt through the skin and in the urine. The symptoms of salt-deficient heat exhaustion normally occur after two or three days of heavy sweating without replacement of salt. The victim may become pallid, collapse, sweat, vomit and sometimes experience cramp in muscle groups. Salt depletion can be avoided by simply taking salt in a water solution. If extra salt is required, dissolve one salt tablet in 1 pint (0.5 l) of water in a water bottle. The solution will not taste salty. When the bottle is refilled add another tablet.

SUNBURN

The prevention of sunburn is very important and is better to apply than the cure. Suitable clothing, such as a cotton shirt with the sleeves worn down, light slacks and a wide-brimmed hat, will protect the skin until a suntan is gradually built up. On very hot sunny days exposure to the direct rays of the sun should be limited. Barrier cream applied to the skin will cut out the harmful ultra-violet rays and so build up a protective tan. Sunburn is a real hazard for the fair-skinned person. His skin can be severely reddened with an irritation which can later change to a burning pain and blistering which may interfere with the secretion of sweat and lead to further complications. In severe cases the patient can become quite ill and develop a headache, fever, occasional vomiting, in addition to the pain of the burn. He can also suffer shock. In such cases obtain expert medical aid. If the sunburn is mild, apply cold wet dressings or calamine lotion for relief then an antiseptic cream at the end of the day.

HEAT STROKE

Heat stroke is the most serious of heat disorders and is caused by a failure of the body's temperature-regulating system. The onset of heat stroke can be sudden. The victim has a very high body temperature but does not perspire so the skin is dry and hot. Preliminary symptoms are similar to those noted for exposure, such as headache, dizziness, restlessness, lack of co-ordination and aggressive behaviour, etc. As the victim's condition deteriorates the disturbances are profound, including delirium, convulsions and partial or complete loss of consciousness with rapid snoring breathing, a fast pulse and a hot, dry, flushed skin. Unless treatment is carried out immediately to check the rise in temperature, coma follows and the victim can die. Treatment in the field should comprise action to reduce his temperature by stripping the victim of his clothing in improvised shade and then sponging him down or covering him with wet towels or wet clothing. Also fan him vigorously. At base he should be immersed in a cool bath that registers 10°C (50°F) which is the best form of treatment. Take note that heat stroke is relatively rare but victims tend to crawl into a quiet spot, such as under the shade of a tree or tent flap, and can escape notice during the critical period of the disorder, sometimes with fatal results.

HEAT EXHAUSTION

Heat exhaustion is caused by a depletion of water and salt. It can be a very serious condition but rarely results in death. The symptoms are numerous and include thirst, profuse sweating, headache, fatigue, confusion, pallor, giddiness, a low urine output; then, if treatment is not started, a state of delirium and coma. Heat exhaustion cases should be treated by re-establishing the water and salt balance through giving drinks of water to which salt has been added. With this treatment and rest in the shade, recovery can be rapid.

PRICKLY HEAT

Prickly heat is caused by the blockage of the sweat glands causing the formation of small blisters which can be seen as tiny, raised irritable areas of the skin. It is a source of great annoyance to the sufferer and will interfere with his sleep. Exercise and more sweating will aggravate the condition. The best cure is to keep in a cool place in the shade and rest.

It is far better to take adequate precautions to avoid heat disorders than to have to apply the cures but the leader of a group that is to trek in hot conditions should familiarize himself with the symptoms of the disorders noted above and also know the cures. The group should be acclimatized to hot conditions before the walk commences and, if possible, should have built up a suntan to counter disorders such as sunburn and prickly heat. The leader should take pains to brief his group on the causes and types of heat disorders and stress how simple it is to avoid them, mainly by an adequate regular intake of water and a prescribed small amount of salt. The leader should check that the group are suitably clad with loose lightweight clothing, permeable to sweat and light in colour so as not to attract the sun's rays. Comfortable, shady hats that cover the head and neck should be worn. Walks should be at a comfortable pace and care taken not to over-tax the group. If need be, they should walk in the early hours to avoid the heat of the day, then rest till the evening before continuing the trek. If the light is strong protect the eyes from the sun's glare by wearing good quality sun-glasses that will reduce the ultra-violet rays but still allow excellent vision.

6
Mountain Safety

Every year thousands of people venture into the hills in search of a challenge and adventure, but, each season, winter or summer, brings its quota of accidents and tragedies. Often the casualties did not appreciate that the hills can at times be both difficult and dangerous, or they had simply not taken the trouble to learn how to deal with potential dangers. When the causes of accidents are analysed they are often found to occur for such reasons as carelessness, overestimating stamina or technical ability, poor observation, lack of knowledge, or failure to act together as a group. However, mountain safety cannot be confined to a set of rules for all the aspects of a trekking expedition are concerned with safety from map and compass technique and load carrying to camp cooking. But safety also concerns the actions of the individual and of the group.

Avoidance of Accidents

Many of the techniques and procedures outlined throughout this book are complementary to mountain safety. It is therefore appropriate to consider the factors that, if observed, would minimize the possibility of an accident occurring on an expedition. Before the expedition commences the leader should ensure that:

(a) the group comprises of at least three persons (see page 78);

(b) the group are adequately trained for the project and the leader is fully aware of the ability of all members, particularly so the weaker members;

(c) the project is carefully planned so as not to overestimate the ability of the group;

(d) the expedition is properly equipped (see Appendix C);

(e) suitable reserve clothing is available to combat weather conditions at their worst;

(f) food is adequate and suitable for the project and emergency rations are also carried;

(g) weather forecasts have been carefully studied;

(h) word has been left of the route to be taken and the estimated time the expedition will be back;
(i) all the group members understand the procedures to adopt in the case of an accident and also the recognized mountain-rescue signals;
(j) the location and telephone numbers of local mountain-rescue units and also of the police are known.

Nevertheless even with well-planned projects accidents can occur and a comparatively simple injury like a sprained knee or twisted ankle can give considerable problems in the mountains, particularly so if the weather commences to deteriorate.

Accident Procedure

In the event of an accident the leader should coolly appraise the situation, check that the casualty is not in immediate danger and the rest of the party are safe. First aid should be rendered at once and the casualty made as comfortable as possible with warmth and shelter arranged. If the injury permits, move him to a sheltered position such as behind a sheep wall or large boulder, and insulate him from cold and damp by using whatever cover is available, such as piled bracken, on which blankets or sleeping bags are laid. If injuries are such that he cannot be moved it will be necessary to construct a shelter around him. This may be achieved by building a wall of stones and then using tent flysheets to give extra protection. Of course, if it is possible to move him into a tent, do so. The casualty and the rest of the group should be reassured so as to reduce and, if possible, eliminate anxiety. The leader has now to decide on the most suitable course of action to adopt and whether to send for help or to evacuate the casualty using improvised equipment to do so. This can be no easy decision to take and the leader will need to consider:

(a) the seriousness of the casualty's injuries;
(b) the physical and mental condition of the remainder of the group;
(c) the weather situation with any indications of weather change;
(d) the access to and ease of a possible escape route;
(e) the location of possible assistance, if required.

SENDING FOR HELP

The decision as to whether to send for help or not can be a difficult one to take. A leader may be reluctant to call out a rescue party as it means demands on volunteers' spare time and perhaps a considerable effort from them. But he must bear in mind that the effects of shock and exhaustion on a casualty can easily be underestimated; therefore whenever there is the possibility that help will be needed it should be sought in good time. If the leader has to err at all it is best if he errs on the side of safety and calls for assistance immediately even when, with hindsight, it may have been possible to have avoided the call-out. He will have made the safest decision that is based on justified concern. If help is required it may be possible to attract local assistance with the aid of a torch, whistle or by shouting for help and using the recognized distress signals noted on page 134.

If the leader decides to send for help, a messenger should be well briefed by the leader on the best route to take, told to descend quickly but carefully and given a note which will explain:

(a) the exact location of the accident with a six-figure map reference and, if possible, the name of nearby landmarks;
(b) the details of the injury;
(c) the number of injured and also the number in the party;
(d) the time of the accident.

If the party is not sure as to their position on a featureless area such as a moor or plateau but can identify features in the distance such as an unmistakeable cairn and church spire that can be recognized on the map, the leader should take a compass bearing on the features and work out the back bearing so that the rescue party can be told the exact point at which the casualty lies. This information is given to the messenger. If the party is of the minimum of three persons, the leader would normally go for help while the other person looks after the casualty. The leader must ensure that the person left is fully briefed as to what treatment to administer to the casualty and any further action that may be required of him. It is very important that the location of the casualty is marked as conspicuously as possible so that the rescue party can locate the bivouac even if conditions are overcast, misty, or dark when they reach the area. A brightly coloured garment such as a red towel or spare day-glow anorak tied to a firmly planted stick or placed on top of a cairn of stones will help locate the casualty. If conditions are dark or very misty the safety rope can also be run out on the ground from the emergency bivouac to attract the attention of the rescuers. Should the very unlikely situation arise where a casualty has to be left on his own, it must be stressed that he must stay where he is. He should be given as much clothing and protection as is possible and be provided with a torch with spare batteries, a bulb and a whistle. Make sure that he has access to food and a fully charged stove, then mark the place well with brightly coloured clothing on a stick or on a cairn of rocks. It must be appreciated that only in the absolute last resort should an unconscious person be left alone. If this drastic action is forced on the leader he should leave a note with the injured person so that if he regains consciousness he will be aware of the rescue action in progress. If the casualty is on exposed steep ground it may be necessary to rope him to a secure point so that he can not roll or fall. However, it should be noted that an injured person, on regaining consciousness, will usually attempt to untie himself.

SIGNALS

When the leader decides that help is required, action should be taken to attract local assistance by using recognized mountain-rescue distress signals. These distress signals can be made with the use of a torch, whistle or by shouting. HELP REQUIRED can be signalled by using the International Alpine Distress Signal: Six flashes, blasts or calls are made in quick succession, followed by a pause of one minute and then the signals are repeated. The International SOS signal comprises three short signals, followed by three longer signals, then three short signals, followed by an interval of one minute. MESSAGE UNDERSTOOD is signalled with three flashes of the lamp or three blasts on a whistle in quick succession followed by a one-minute interval. It is traditional that those people who use the hills and mountains for pleasure are the first to offer help in the event of an accident and assist official Mountain Rescue Teams. A knowledge of some additional signals agreed for use in mountain rescue is therefore necessary. RETURN TO BASE can be signalled with a lamp or whistle by a prolonged succession of flashes or blasts. If flares are used a red flare signifies help needed, a white flare can be used to signal message understood or for illumination purposes, and a green flare to recall rescue units to base. The position of a mountain-rescue base camp may be marked by white or yellow flares or a continuous light.

It is extremely important that when signals are seen or heard the location is immediately noted by the rescuers and recorded with a compass bearing taken on the position of the signal. If possible, obtain two bearings from different positions so as to pinpoint the precise position of the signal being transmitted.

EVACUATING THE CASUALTY

To attempt to carry a casualty some distance across mountainous terrain is a very tiring undertaking, particularly as great care is necessary so as not to jolt or cause the casualty further discomfort. At the minimum four men are needed to carry a person and with frequent reliefs. Even when the assistance of six men is available the task can still be very hard and exhausting. It should be borne in mind that mountain-rescue teams are trained in movement over rough ground with a casualty and they have the experience, technique and support in man-power to cater for such difficulties. The leader should therefore appreciate that, with a small group, the difficulties of carrying a casualty on an improvised seat or stretcher over some distance are considerable, can be extremely exhausting and even dangerous. Improvised carrys are therefore of use for moving an injured person to a sheltered position or evacuating, over a comparatively short distance, a casualty whose injuries are of a minor nature. They should only be used otherwise for evacuation purposes when it is considered that the danger to the casualty is greater if he were to remain where he is on the mountain.

BASIC CARRYS

Methods of carrying by hand with the support of one or two people are practicable for movement over a very short distance only as they can be extremely exhausting unless the casualty is very light and the supporter(s) very strong. Take note that freedom from pain is much more important than a speedy evacuation and this fact, plus the realization that the casualty must be kept warm all the time to offset the effects of shock and exposure, must be uppermost in the leader's mind. These considerations should influence the leader's decision as to whether he should await a rescue team or attempt to evacuate the casualty and, if so, the method to be used. Some improvised methods of carrying are as follows:

One Man

(a) *Piggy-back.* The piggy-back carry is the simplest but the most exhausting. The casualty is placed on the back of the carrier who supports the casualty's thighs (Fig. 96).

FIG. 96 The piggy-back carry is simple but exhausting.

(b) *Fireman's Lift.* The carrier brings the casualty's left arm over his

FIG. 97 The fireman's lift, suitable over short distances.

right shoulder from behind and passes his left arm between the casualty's legs to hoist him on to his shoulder (Fig. 97).

(c) *Rucksack Carry.* A rucksack can be turned into a carrying aid by cutting slits in either side to take the casualty's legs so that he is carried on the back of the supporter. The casualty can also be carried with his legs through the fully extended straps of the empty rucksack (Fig. 98).

FIG. 98 One method of rucksack carry. The casualty sits on the empty sack with his legs through the fully extended rucksack straps.

(d) *Split-rope Carry.* The one-man split-rope carry utilizes the safety rope which is separated into two coils. The carrier's arms run through each coil like the straps of a rucksack. The casualty passes his legs through the coils which are drawn together with several loops to make a secure seat and is supported on the back of the carrier (Fig. 99).

FIG. 99 The split-rope carry uses the safety rope separated into two coils drawn together with loops. The rope is padded for comfort.

Two Man

(e) *Pole Carry.* Two carriers are employed and a strong pole is slotted

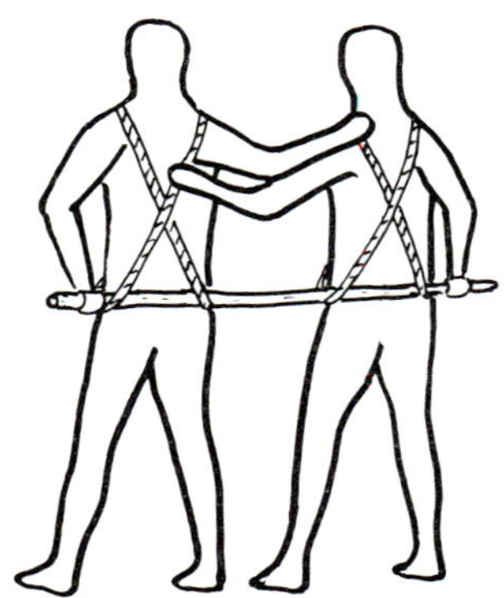

FIG. 100 The two-man pole carry requires the use of cross slings or main rucksack straps to support a stout pole which is padded for comfort.

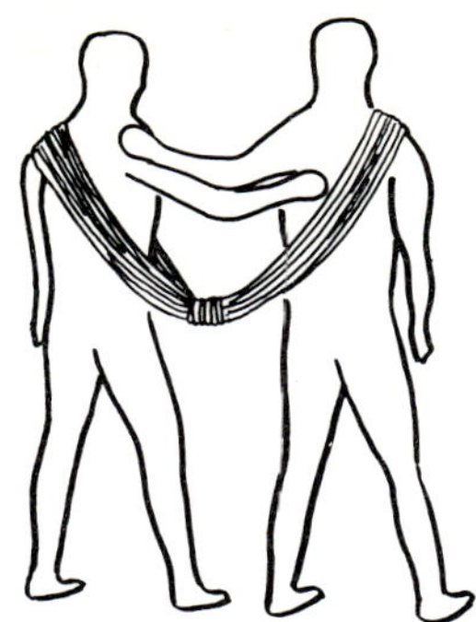

FIG. 101 The two-man split rope carry uses a rescue rope coiled to form large loops.

through their main rucksack straps, or through crossed rope slings at waist height (Fig. 100). The casualty then sits on the pole, which is padded to give extra comfort, between the two carriers.

(f) *Two-man Split-rope Carry.* A rescue rope is coiled with large loops so that it will drape over the outside shoulders of the two carriers who stand close together. Several small loops around the ropes keep the coils together in the centre. The casualty then sits on the padded rope with his back supported by the inner arm of each carrier. (Fig. 101).

IMPROVISED STRETCHERS

It is easier to carry a casualty on a proper rigid stretcher than by any of the basic carrys noted above or the methods described below. However, in an emergency the leader may have to improvise and the following sub-paragraphs describe how to make do with the rescue rope alone, and using poles and anoraks to form an emergency stretcher:

(a) *The Piggott Rope Stretcher.* This form of improvised stretcher can be made from a 100-ft (30-m) (or longer) safety rope. Six yards/metres of rope are left free, then eight loops are made about a hand's span apart and 3 ft (1 m) long which are tied off with an overhand knot (Fig. 102). Sheet-bend knots are tied down the other side and loops made at the corners. The free end of the rope is run down the middle so as to give extra support under the casualty and is tied at each cross point with an overhand

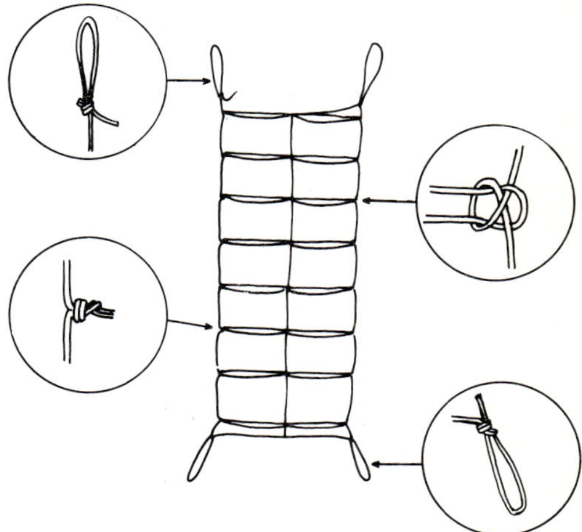

FIG. 102 The Piggott rope stretcher can be made from a 100-ft (30-m) (or longer) safety rope. Overhand and sheetbend knots are employed.

knot. Four persons can carry the casualty, but the number can be increased to six if hand loops are tied halfway along the stretcher, one on either side. Take note that the Piggott stretcher should not be used if there is a possibility of spinal injury to the casualty.

(b) *Pole/Anorak Stretcher.* Two anoraks are used with their sleeves pushed inside out. Two strong poles are slid through the sleeves so that the anoraks form a canvas bed. If available, lash two strong crossmembers with diagonal lashings near either end to hold the frame firm. A more comfortable bed can be made if spare sweaters are laid on the anoraks. Four persons carry the stretcher, two at each end, but if it is possible to cross-lash two long, strong crossmembers one at either end, additional support can also be given on the crossmembers.

(c) *Pole/Anorak Sedan.* In this method the casualty is carried sitting upright (Fig. 103). The sleeves of an anorak are turned inside out and two poles are slid through the arm holes. The poles are then slotted through the straps of the front carrier's rucksack or through rope cross slings and gripped by the front carrier. The casualty sits with his back to the rucksack of the front carrier. Two other carriers, one on either side, support the poles at the rear.

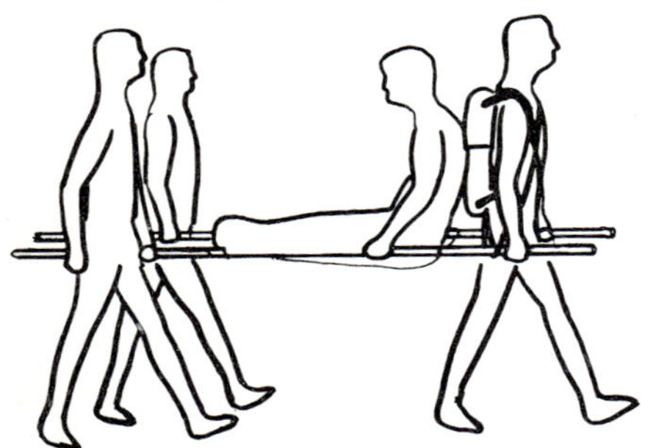

FIG. 103 The pole/anorak sedan. The poles are slotted through the front man's crossed slings or run through his rucksack straps.

Procedure When Lost in the Hills

In the event of a group becoming lost the leader must ensure that the party remains calm and stays together. He should, if possible, find a nearby sheltered spot, then sit down and, while the group rests, carefully work out their position from visible landmarks if these are available. He may need to assess their approximate position by working out the time taken from a known feature previously passed, using Naismith's formula. The leader must now decide whether the party should go on or stop where it is. If the weather is bad or misty, or if darkness is descending, it may be best to bivouac until morning. Take note that map reading and navigating in the dark are very difficult as it may be impossible when walking to distinguish between a sudden depression in the ground and a precipice, so it is normally far wiser to make camp for the night. If tents are carried, camp should be established, warm clothes put on and a hot meal prepared. If the party does not possess tents or conditions are such that it is impossible to erect tents then each person should get out of the wind, put on spare clothing with warm dry clothes next to the skin and insulate the body further by sitting on a rucksack or rope. Better protection can be obtained from sitting on the rope and placing the feet and hands in the rucksack, the sleeve of which is pulled out to give added cover. A 500-gauge or thicker polythene industrial bag with breathing holes cut in the top should be carried by each person on a high-level expedition. This can be pulled right over the head and will give excellent protection to the body from wind and rain (Fig. 104). Emergency bivouac sacks can in fact be purchased made of 500-gauge polythene coloured bright orange for safety and measuring 48 x 96 ins (120 x 240 cm); other plastic survival bags are available in bright orange and measure 3 ft x 6 ft 6 ins (91 x 198 cm). There is also a selection of 'space' blankets retailed, made of aluminized plastic and fibre, that have the property of giving excellent insulation to the body with up to 90 per cent of body heat reflected by the blanket. If conditions are very cold keep awake by exercising the hands, arms and legs and even wiggle the toes. It is also important that clothing does not restrict the circulation as this could, in very cold conditions, possibly lead to frostbite and bring on exposure. A warm meal and hot drinks will also help to retain body heat.

FIG. 104 In an emergency bivouac situation get out of the wind, put on dry clothing, sit on the rope and use the rucksack with the sleeve drawn out to protect the hands, thighs and legs. A large, 500-gauge (or thicker) polythene bag, with holes cut to allow you to breathe, will give excellent protection.

Bivouacs

A well-organized trekking group intent on walking for several days should always carry suitable tents to provide comfort and also good protection in the event of bad weather. However, a knowledge of how to bivouac using basic materials such as an old flysheet, polythene sheet or polythene bag is highly desirable as mountain weather is known to be extremely fickle and difficulties can be experienced even on a one-day walk.

A bivouac is a form of simple shelter that will afford protection for the night. It can be constructed from natural materials such as straw, reeds, leaves and saplings but this form of construction is only possible at protected low-level sites. Any strong, closely woven canvas can be used to make a bivouac, but a light waterproof fabric is preferable. Proofed cotton fabric, similar to that used in a lightweight tent, being 3 oz (85 g) to the square yard (metre) in weight, is ideal. An old but serviceable flysheet is suitable provided it has retained its waterproof qualities, though the flysheet can be treated with Mesowax to regain these properties if they have been lost. Tie tapes sewn to the edges and in the middle of the sheet will ensure that the cover can easily be securely attached to a firm point. A good bivouac needs a fair amount of thought in its construction. You want to be well protected and comfortable, and know full well that if the wind increases or there is heavy rain in the night it will not worry you unduly. When you site the bivouac consider the direction of the prevailing wind, then secure the canvas firmly to branches, pegs, stones or whatever medium of attachment is available to keep it erect and in shape. If this is not done you may be exposed to uncomfortable draughts or directly to the wind. It is important that the body is well insulated from the dampness in the ground so, if possible, lay a bed of dry heather, bracken, light branches or leaves where you will lie. Also consider which way you will lie within the bivouac. Your head should normally be at the snuggest part – the closed end. Bivouacs can take many

FIG. 105 A bivouac constructed against the leeward side of a sheep wall.

forms. A sheep wall will offer excellent protection when trekking the moors, for a bivouac can be constructed against the leeward side of a wall and secured in place by heavy stones laid on the edge of the fabric (Fig. 105). During summer it is possible to enjoy a good night's rest in deep heather by simply securing the edges of a bivouac sheet very firmly to the ground with suitable stones, or pegs. If you tie the sheet to heather roots make sure that they are very strongly embedded in the ground. The heather is soft to sleep on and the sheet will keep the early morning dew off your sleeping bag and also give protection against any breeze during the night. In a mountain forest or at low level a bivouac can be made by selecting two trees just over 6 ft (180 cm) apart, with a suitable clear area between them. A mattress of light branches and twigs is laid between the two trees and the bedding of either a Klondike Roll or sleeping bag is laid on top. A strong piece of string is run around the bole of one tree to the other and tied so that it is taut and about 2 ft (60 cm) off the ground. A plastic sheet or other suitable cover is then laid over the string to make a small 'A' ridge shape; the string supporting the ridge roof. The material is pulled out on either side and pegged to the ground with pieces of branch or held down with logs or stones. The plastic is pierced at each end next to the bole of the tree so that both ends can be closed as far as possible with pieces of string, or lines can be run from tie tapes on a canvas sheet. Figs 106-110 outline some other methods of bivouacking.

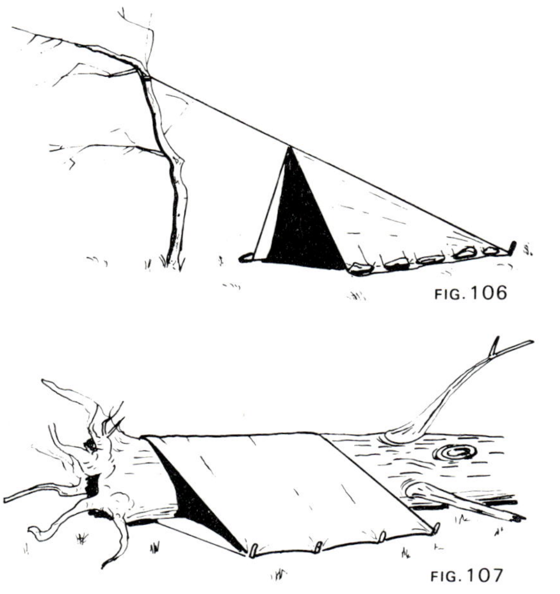

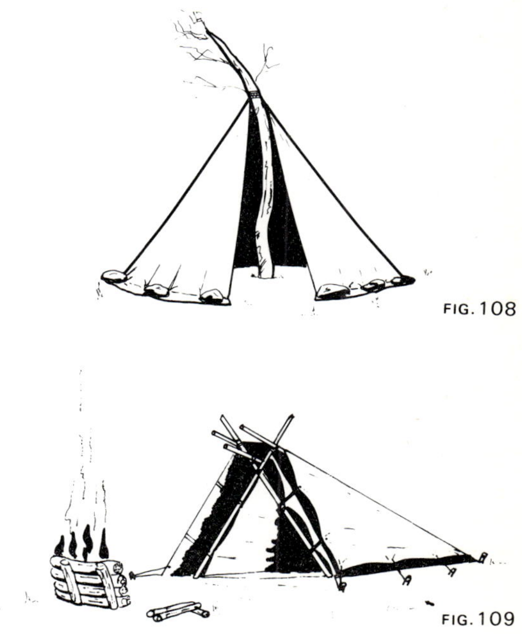

FIG. 106 A simple bivouac using a tree for support and erected backing into the wind.

FIG. 107 Even a felled tree trunk will afford protection; secure the bivouac sheet with pegs on both sides.

FIG. 108 A teepee-type bivouac using a tree.

FIG. 109 A double-walled bivouac gives good protection. The fire shown is the reflector type.

FIG. 110 This more elaborate shelter based on the American canoe bivouac uses tie tapes to lift the canvas and obtain maximum internal space. A gin pole supports the mess-can over an economical, slow-burning, lazyman's fire.

Natural Way-finding

In an emergency it is possible in certain conditions to navigate without the aid of a compass by using the sun or stars or other traditional way-finding methods such as observing the growth pattern of trees or the position of moss on boulders or trees.

A wrist watch can be used to navigate by the sun. First of all stand with your left shoulder towards the sun and hold your watch flat on the palm of the left hand. Now move the watch around until the hour hand points directly towards the sun. South can be located by finding the halfway point between the hour hand and 12 o'clock the shortest way forward if it is morning and counter-clockwise, that is backwards, if the afternoon. If you are on any form of daylight-saving time be sure to take this into consideration. It is more difficult to find south on a cloudy day, but you can do so by standing a match or small twig upright alongside the watch and then move both about until the shadow of the match or twig falls directly on the hour hand. The hour hand is now pointing directly towards the sun and you proceed to find south as before.

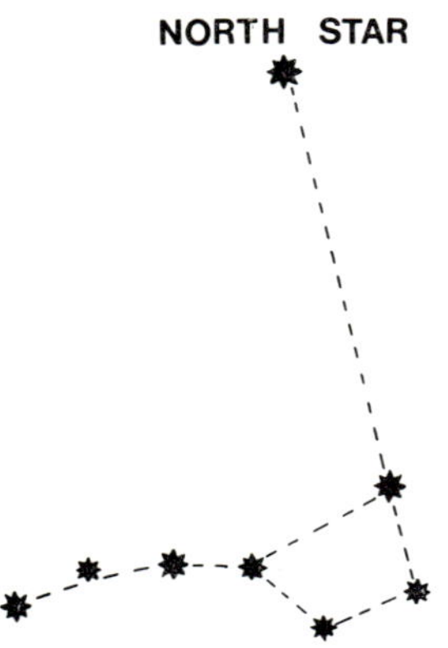

FIG. 111 In the northern hemisphere true north can be found from the constellation of the Great Bear which points to Polaris (North Star).

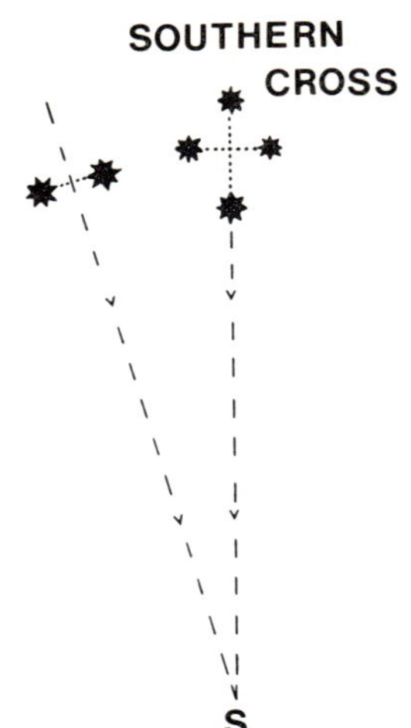

FIG. 112 In the southern hemisphere, the Southern Cross indicates south.

Another and more accurate way to find south is to note at 12.00 hours the position of the shadow cast by an object that is perpendicular to the ground. In the northern hemisphere the base of the shadow will indicate south and the tip north. On a clear night in the northern hemisphere true north can be found from the constellation of the Great Bear which points to Polaris (the North Star) located over the north pole. (Fig. 111). In the southern hemisphere the Southern Cross indicates the direction of south (Fig. 112).

Natural methods of direction finding can be used in the mountains although they are normally more effective at lower level where there is more vegetation. In some areas prevailing winds can be strong and influence the growth of the trees so that their growth pattern is away from the direction of the prevailing wind. As the direction of the wind should be known the approximate direction of south can be located by studying the shape of the trees. Where hill and mountain forests are growing in more sheltered areas the top branches of spruce and pine usually point slightly south east and towards the rising sun. However, this is not so in exposed areas or deep valleys. In the former case strong winds will influence the growth of the branches. In the latter the height of the surrounding hills can shade early morning sunshine and there is therefore no growth reaction from the top branches.

Trees usually grow thickest and more luxuriantly on the sunny side, the south side. If you look at the trunk of a cut down tree you will see that the annual rings are usually wider and the bark thickest on the northern or north-east aspect of the trunk. However, have a good look at several such trees and take the average pattern of growth.

It is commonly held that moss grows on the north side of a tree or boulder. Take note that moss will grow on any side of a tree or boulder where there is moisture. Moss on trees that have unusually rough areas on the bark or on those that lean or are broken should not be considered. Care must be taken not to mistake the moss for the grey-green lichen that is often found on trees and rocks. Also ignore the moss that grows at the base of the tree; it grows there all the year round. So, to be as accurate as possible, consider only straight trees having a fairly smooth surface which do not grow in densely wooded areas where they can be shaded on one or all sides. The trees to check are those that are exposed to the sun's rays and are not in a shady copse. Moss that is found on these trees will be on one side only, the north side. This is because the sun hardly reaches the northern aspect of the tree as it moves from sunrise to sunset and so the moss cannot be burnt off. However, do not be satisfied until you have inspected several trees in the area and not just one.

It must be appreciated that natural way-finding methods are only an emergency means of navigation and cannot in any way compare with the high degree of accuracy that is provided by the compass.

7
Weather

A mountain walker should have a basic knowledge of the weather in order to interpret local weather signs and so anticipate changes in the weather. In mountainous areas local weather conditions are liable to alter rapidly and at times even dramatically. On high land changeable weather can bring unseasonal conditions, such as snow in summer and sunny mild days in winter. The leader of an expedition should therefore, in the interest of safety, at all times ensure that his group are equipped for bad weather conditions. However, generally speaking weather forecasts from the radio, TV and the newspapers are reliable and, when combined with careful observation of local weather conditions, should enable the leader to predict the weather with reasonable accuracy and plan his programme accordingly. The object of this chapter is to give the reader a basic understanding of the weather.

The main reason for variations in weather is the movement of air caused by differences in temperature over the earth's surface due to the sun's heat. These air movements are complicated by the presence of large land masses, high mountains, oceans and also by the fact that the earth rotates on its axis. The weather in many areas of the world follows a set pattern with seasonal periods of sunshine, rain and snow. Even the wind can have patterns of direction and strength according to the season. However, the weather in other parts of the world, and particularly in mountainous regions, can be irregular. European weather does not have the same stability as some other parts due to the effects of a number of air masses. Air masses initially acquire their qualities by stagnating over a region of origin for several days, perhaps over a very hot desert or polar area. These air masses are described according to their source of origin as tropical, equatorial, arctic or polar. Europe is influenced by arctic, continental polar, maritime polar, maritime tropical and continental tropical air masses. Arctic air is bitterly cold in winter and also cold in summer. If it reaches Europe from the north the warm sea influences the air mass and it becomes unstable bringing showers and snow in winter. The north of the continent of Europe has quite high summer temperatures so continental polar air is dry and fairly warm in summer but cold in winter. Maritime polar air, even in winter, is comparatively mild because it crosses and is influenced by the warm North Atlantic. In summer it is cool and brings showers. Maritime tropical air is mild in winter and in summer it is cool and cloudy but also humid and often foggy. Continental tropical air brings dry warm air to Europe from the Sahara. In winter it makes for pleasant mild conditions and in summer gives rise to heat waves.

The principal air masses over North America are similar to those in Europe. West of the Rockies they have similar properties to European air masses. However, the Rockies effect a barrier running from north to south so that in winter arctic and continental polar air sweeps southwards to cause very cold conditions. North America is also affected by other air masses. Warm, moist maritime tropical air flows north-west from the Gulf of Mexico and can give rise to heavy rain. The Atlantic is cold off the north-east coast and the maritime polar air masses are therefore colder than over Europe.

The weather has several basic elements that are of particular interest to the mountain walker; these are wind, cloud, temperature and humidity.

Wind

Air behaves the same way as water and moves from areas of high pressure to areas where the pressure is lower. The greater the difference in air pressure between two places the faster the air will move and the stronger the wind will blow.

The direction of the wind can give an indication of the type of weather to expect. Winds blowing across Great Britain from the south and south-west are likely to be warm as they can blow from the warm regions of the sub-Tropics. However, as they cross the Atlantic they are normally moist and can give rain, as may a west wind. A wind from the north, on the other hand, is likely to blow cold air across the country and may be very cold having originated in the polar areas. Winds from the east blowing across Europe are often dry and, in winter, cold.

The prevailing wind is that wind that occurs most often. Over much of North America and Western Europe it is westerly but in the Tropics and the Caribbean it is generally easterly. The growth pattern of vegetation such as trees and bushes is often influenced by the prevailing wind for the angle of growth can be affected. As stated in Chapter 6, in an emergency situation where no compass is available observation of the growth pattern and a knowledge of the direction of the prevailing wind can help you identify the correct course to take.

The effects of the wind on the body can be considerable. At a given temperature the air feels cooler if there is a breeze than if conditions are still. The stronger the breeze the greater its cooling effect and in high wind conditions the cooling is very considerable. At low temperature this effect is called 'wind chill' and when cold and wet conditions are combined, the effect on the human body can be extremely dangerous. Temperatures far below freezing are tolerable in calm conditions but can become lethal in strong winds. A temperature of 27°-32°F (-3-0°C) in still conditions will produce a slight frost and nippy though not unpleasant conditions for the winter camper; but if the wind is strong the frost will be severe and camping out becomes a much more rigorous and testing exercise. Winds at sea level are often gusty but not of any great strength. However, winds at altitude become stronger due to the absence of friction with the earth's surface and are also steadier. The speed of the wind on an open moor at an elevation of 3,000 ft (900 m) is in the region of 2½ times the speed in sheltered areas at about sea level. Thus a gentle breeze of 12 mph (19 km/h) (see Beaufort Scale, Fig. 113) at sea level will increase to 30 mph (48 km/h) at 3,000 ft (900 m) and register as a strong breeze. Similarly, a fresh breeze of 20 mph (32 km/h) at sea level will, at 3,000 ft (900 m), increase to a strong gale. It should be noted that forecast wind strengths are normally given for sea level or near sea-level conditions. It is therefore very important that the leader takes this fact into consideration when he plans to walk at some height.

Clouds

Clouds form as level sheets, lumpy masses of vapour, or as a combination of the two. Cloud formations are often associated with a particular kind of weather and noting changes in their formation can give vital clues to the weather on the way. First of all, let us look at the three basic cloud types:

Type: Cirrus (CI).
Group: High cloud, 5-9 miles (8-14 km) up.
Characteristics: White, composed of ice crystals; may take the form of fine feathery strands which may be twisted at the ends like 'mare's tails'.
Predicts: If still or very slow moving in an otherwise blue sky, usually indicates fine weather continuing. If increasing in amount and moving relatively quickly it means rain or snow on the way although this may be 24

Wind Speed mph	*Beaufort Scale*	*Wind Force*	*Description*
1	0	Calm	Smoke rises vertically.
1 - 3	1	Light air	Wind direction shown by smoke and not by wind vane.
4 - 7	2	Slight breeze	Wind felt on face, leaves rustle, ordinary vane moves.
8 - 12	3	Gentle breeze	Leaves and small twigs in constant motion, wind extends high flag.
13 - 18	4	Moderate breeze	Raises dust and loose paper, small branches are moved, snow begins to drift.
19 - 24	5	Fresh breeze	Small trees in leaf begin to sway, created wavelets form on inland waters.
25 - 31	6	Strong breeze	Large branches in motion, whistling heard in telegraph wires, high snow-drifts occur.
32 - 38	7	High wind	Whole trees in motion, some difficulty in walking against wind, visibility obscured by drifting snow.
39 - 46	8	Gale	Breaks twigs off trees, generally slows progress.
47 - 54	9	Strong gale	Slight structural damage occurs, chimney pots and slates fall off roofs.
55 - 63	10	Whole gale	Inland trees uprooted.
64 - 72	11	Storm	Widespread damage.
73 - 82	12	Hurricane	Hurricane.

FIG. 113 The Beaufort Scale.

hours or so away. Take note that cirrus clouds may appear slow moving but this is only because of their height. They normally approach from the south-west or north-west.

Type: Cumulus (CU).
Group: Base, usually low, but the tops can tower to 20,000 ft (6000 m) or more.
Characteristics: Like a heap of cotton wool, dark at the base and rising to a white dome. When it towers to a great height it develops a cirrus-like top which spreads out into an 'anvil' shape – the cloud is then called cumulonimbus (CB).
Predicts: Small, fluffy drifting cumulus clouds indicate fine weather. As the clouds get bigger the chance of sudden showers increases. Cumulus usually increase in size and number over hills and correspondingly so does the intensity and frequency of showers. The very large cumulonimbus clouds often herald thunderstorms on a summer's evening and, over high ground in Britain, are associated with snow and hail showers in winter and spring. There are two flatter sorts of cloud in this group, stratocumulus (SC) and altocumulus (AC). They take the form of many globules in patches in the sky which may be light grey near the centre but white at the edges or even cover the whole sky. Patchy altocumulus on a summer's day may be innocuous, but if the clouds start to sprout little 'cauliflower heads' there is a risk of thundery rain. Stratocumulus is like a patchwork of flattened cumulus, soft in outline, grey in colour and often associated with quiet weather at any time of the year, but light rain or snow may fall, more especially in winter.

Type: Stratus (ST).
Group: Normally low or very low but can form at any height.
Characteristics: Usually a uniform featureless grey base which can form right down to the ground. Fog is really stratus at ground level. Sometimes the stratus can be 1,000 ft (300 m) or more, thick and probably merge into stratocumulus above. In the medium levels, altostratus (AS) may form and this can be seen as a bluish sheet or layer, fibrous or uniform in appearance. It has a base around 8,000-14,000 ft (2500-4200 m) and

can give the sun or moon a 'watery' appearance. Cirrostratus (CS) is a high, uniform cirrus layer which often produces a halo around the sun or moon.

Predicts: Hills are often covered in stratus when the surrounding low lands have good visibility. Stratus may be just hill fog with only a little drizzle, but it is often present below a dense mass of cloud when a front or depression is in the vicinity. Both cirrostratus and altostratus are usually forerunners of worsening weather. The sequence of clouds ahead of a depression or active 'warm front' is as follows (see Fig. 117). First of all any cumulus that may have been about appear to flatten into stratocumulus and disappear as cirrus increases usually from a westerly direction. Then cirrostratus appear and a halo may be seen around the sun or moon. Altostratus clouds now form, sometimes with altocumulus, and the altostratus base steadily lowers until rain starts. Eventually the altostratus base comes down to 4,000 ft (1200 m) or less and it is then called nimbostratus (NS). Often low stratus and stratocumulus will occur below this and the unwary walker will find himself in hill fog. Usually during this sequence the wind will back and freshen.

Summary of clouds
Scattered cirrus clouds which show little movement in a blue sky usually mean good weather continuing. Cumulus clouds in general indicate sunny periods and showers. Remember that the bigger the cloud the heavier and more frequent the showers will be. Small cumulus will rarely give showers. 'Flat' cloud, such as stratocumulus, may well be innocuous and stratus may just be hill fog, but increasing and lowering layer cloud is always a sign of an impending deterioration in conditions, especially in hill regions. If cumulus clouds appear to be getting flatter it usually means that showers will die away and the wind will drop, at least temporarily. However, this sequence is sometimes followed quickly by the lowering layer cloud sequence so keep a watch out as the improvement may not last long. Quite often the sky will contain a mixture of cloud types and it is as well to notice whether any particular type is increasing, decreasing or newly appearing as this may give clues as suggested above.

Temperature

Noting changes in temperature along with other information can be of value in predicting the weather. If a thermometer is available, place it in the shade and away from direct sunlight in order to get a good idea of the air temperature. The temperature that one 'feels' may be misleading due to conditions of wind and sun or lack of these, and also to humidity. A sunny and relatively calm day in spring may feel warm but the air temperature is often deceptively low. If it is below about 50°F (10°C) in early afternoon, then a chilly night is in prospect, with frost a possibility. You should not go unprepared for chilly conditions even when the temperature is reasonably high. Remember that as well as the drop in temperature as you climb there can be an increase in wind with the accompanying wind-chill effect.

Cooled air contracts, sinks and sheds moisture. Warm air expands, rises and carries moisture. During still conditions, and particularly in anti-cyclones, cold air will sink into valleys and onto low ground, both in winter and summer, and fog may form. Dependent on the time of year frost may also occur. This change in temperature is known as 'temperature inversion'.

As previously stated, air moves from areas where the pressure is high to where it is lower. Air pressure is often lower over hot regions than it is over cooler regions. This is often so near the sea, for on a hot day a breeze will blow from off the cool water to the hot land. At night the land cools and the reverse will take place so that the breeze will now blow from the land to the sea. Air temperature over mountains reduces the higher the altitude. This drop in temperature is known as the 'lapse rate'. In dry air conditions this decrease is about 5°F (3°C) per 1,000 ft (300 m), in humid conditions the decrease is about 4°F (2°C) per 1,000 ft (300 m). Therefore if we have a dry airstream with a temperature at sea level of 10°F (6°C), the temperature at 2,000 ft (600 m) will be at freezing point.

Humidity

Water vapour is always present in the air. This water is derived by evaporation from oceans, lakes, rivers, soil, and trees and other vegetation and is termed humidity. A perpetual interchange is taking place with the air drawing moisture from the earth to form clouds which eventually pour the moisture back onto the earth as rain or snow. We are seldom aware of the moisture in the air except on a hot, sultry day when the humidity of the air is high and conditions are moist and damp, and perspiration cannot evaporate from our bodies. Such conditions feel oppressive. In winter time high humidity makes for muggy or raw conditions. If the humidity is low the air is said to be dry and conditions feel brisk and invigorating.

It is more likely to rain when the humidity of the air is high than when the humidity is low. Air that is in contact with the surface of the earth gradually acquires the humidity and the temperature of the land. If such an air mass moves as an airstream the countries over which it flows will be affected by the humidity contained within the airstream. Due to the properties of air masses the mild tropical maritime airstream reaching Great Britain from the west or south-west is usually very moist, especially in south-west Britain where much hill fog will occur, although it may dry out sufficiently in crossing the country to give sunshine in eastern districts. Alternatively, a very dry polar continental airstream will give clear skies nearly everywhere in Great Britain if it arrives from the south-east having had a short sea-track across the Channel. However, if it arrives from the east or north-east, having crossed the North Sea it tends to have picked up enough moisture to give a lot of cloud in north-east England and can, on occasions in winter, lead to a considerable snowfall in the Pennines.

Weather Forecast Charts

A weather forecast chart or weather map will have lines on the map that join places of equal pressure; these are isobars (Figs 114 and 115). Each isobar may be marked with the height of the barometer in inches, such as 29.53 ins which would equate to 1000 millibars (mb). Isobars form patterns identifiable as depressions and anti-cyclones. Fronts mark the boundaries between air masses and usually lie across the isobars. A

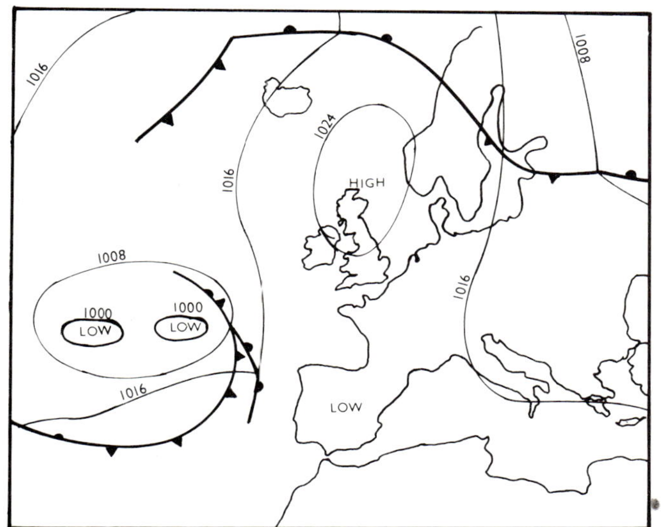

FIG. 114 An Atlantic weather map. The heavy lines with spikes indicate a cold front; those with half circles a warm front. The occluded front has a cold and warm front joined together and therefore has spikes and half circles. Note the anti-cyclone located over the United Kingdom.

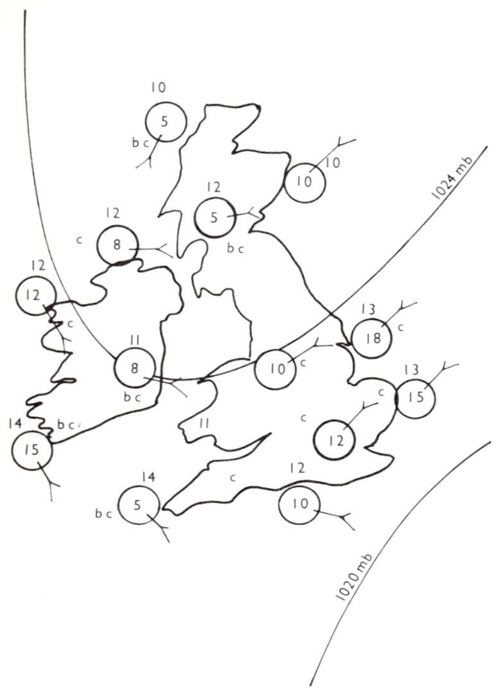

FIG. 115 A British Isles forecast map. This map is related to the Atlantic weather map in Fig. 114. The anti-cyclone centred over the United Kingdom will give dry conditions, particularly in the north. Arrows show the wind direction, and the figures in circles indicate windspeed in mph. Take note that the flow of the wind in an anti-cyclone or high in the northern hemisphere is always in a clockwise direction. The figures outside the circles give the temperatures (°C). Symbols on weather maps include the following: b – blue sky; bc – half clouded; c – cloudy; o – overcast; f – fog; d – drizzle; h – hail; m – mist; r – rain; s – snow; tir – thunderstorms; p – showers; mb – millibars.

depression is an area of low atmospheric pressure. Some smaller depressions move quickly and have characteristic features of wind, temperature, cloud and humidity which help identification. Wind direction is shown on the map by the figure denoting the speed in miles per hour within a circle (Fig. 115). The direction of the wind is shown by an arrow attached to the circle. Some weather maps have a direction arrow with the wind speed alongside. When winds blow from a high-pressure area to a low they do not flow in a straight line but take a spiral course. In the northern hemisphere winds in depressions blow in an anti-clockwise direction and partially inwards across the isobars. By noting the direction and strength of the wind it is possible to identify the various stages of a passing depression and your position in relation to the system. To find the direction in which the centre lies stand with your back to the wind; the depression, or 'low' as it is also called, will be on your left. This is known as 'Buys Ballot's Law'. Its application can be seen in Figs 116A and B where a depression is crossing an area and moving in a north-easterly direction. The observer at X will initially experience a south-easterly wind, then a period of light and variable wind as the centre moves directly over, followed by a freshening north-westerly wind as the low moves away. The closer together the isobars, the stronger will be the wind. A trough of low pressure, frequently referred to in weather forecasts, is formed as a depression commences and is shown on the

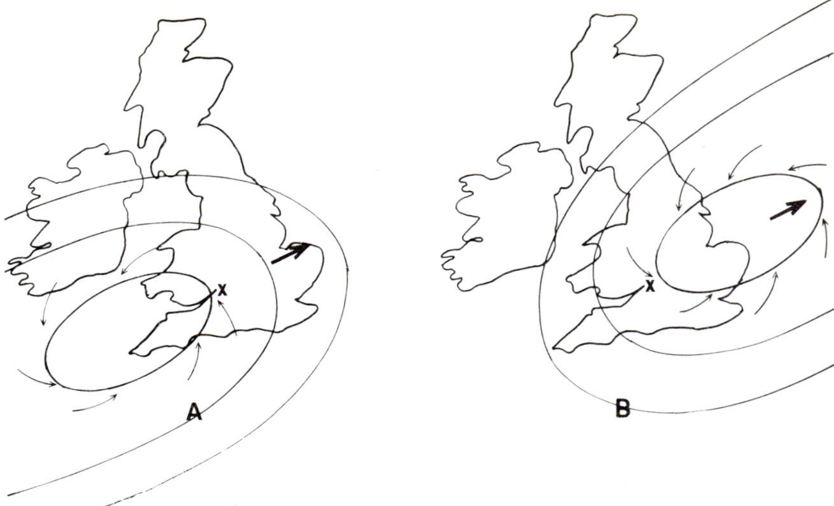

FIG. 116 A depression moving north-east. Note that the wind in a depression in the northern hemisphere blows in an anti-clockwise direction. A – as the depression approaches an observer at X, the wind will blow at that point from the direction of south-east. In B the depression has moved further north-east and the wind blows at point X from the direction of north-west.

weather map as a pattern of V-shaped isobars making a valley with low pressure inside. These troughs are often associated with fronts, particularly those of an active developing depression. Ahead of such a trough the wind is usually southerly or south-westerly over Great Britain veering to north-westerly behind it.

An anti-cyclone or 'high' is an area of high pressure. It is shown on a map by a central closed isobar usually much larger than the central isobar of a depression. It often gives quiet static conditions and the winds, which are usually light, blow (in the northern hemisphere) in a clockwise direction around it. Sometimes the skies are relatively cloud free but, often in winter and occasionally in summer, there is an overcast of stratocumulus cloud from which drizzle or light snow may fall. When cloud is absent, night fog on low ground is common, particularly in autumn and winter, but the hills may have little or no fog. A ridge of high pressure is a wedge-shaped extension of an anti-cyclone or a belt of high pressure connecting two anti-cyclones. The conditions in the ridge are similar to those in an anti-cyclone but are usually of shorter duration. The presence of the ridge can be identified by the drop in the wind.

Fronts are boundaries between different air masses which tend to move bodily and not mix easily with one another. A cold front means cold air is advancing and pushing back warm air and a warm front is similarly warm air advancing, pushing back cold air. The depressions in temperate latitudes have a warm front followed by a cold front. The air in between is the 'warm sector'. Eventually the cold front overtakes the warm and the warm air is lifted off the ground. This process is called occlusion and the boundary between the two 'cold' air masses at the surface is called an occluded front. These fronts are shown on the weather map by heavy lines, with triangles indicating a cold front, half circles a warm front and a combination of the two for an occluded front (Fig. 114). The symbols are placed on the side towards which the front is moving. The forecast temperatures on the weather map show that the temperature is higher in the warm sector than elsewhere. The humidity is also higher.

The sequence of cloud development ahead of a warm front was described in the section on clouds, briefly summarized as an increase and lowering of layer clouds until a steady rain or snow commences (Fig. 117). There is often a backing and freshening of the wind as the front appoaches. With the passage of a warm front the steady rain will usually cease and a light drizzle ensue. The temperature and humidity will rise. The visibility may well become poorer and the wind will veer and usually decrease in strength. However, this is not always so. Although sometimes the weather will clear for a time in the warm sector, there are occasions, especially in the hills of western Britain, where heavy rain may continue in the warm sector due to 'orographic uplift'. The very moist air is lifted sufficiently on hitting the hills to make its moisture condense and fall as substantial rainfall. The cold front will often follow the warm front within 12-24 hours or less, but occasionally the warm sector can last several days and rain may continue in the hills throughout this period, perhaps giving substantial falls, whilst in the sheltered lowlands just a little drizzle may be all that occurs.

Assuming that we are in a 'normal' warm sector with low cloud and drizzle, the approach of the cold front is heralded by a period of more continuous rain usually of shorter duration than that ahead of the warm front, but sometimes quite heavy for a short spell (Fig. 118). Above the stratus the layer clouds will have increased again and sometimes a cumulonimbus may be embedded in them which will give rise to the heavy burst of rain and occasional thunder may occur. As the cold air arrives there is usually a fall in temperature and in humidity, accompanied by a veering of the wind. The rain may well cease but sometimes carries on for a while behind the cold front. However, looking upwind you will see the cloud breaking, and in

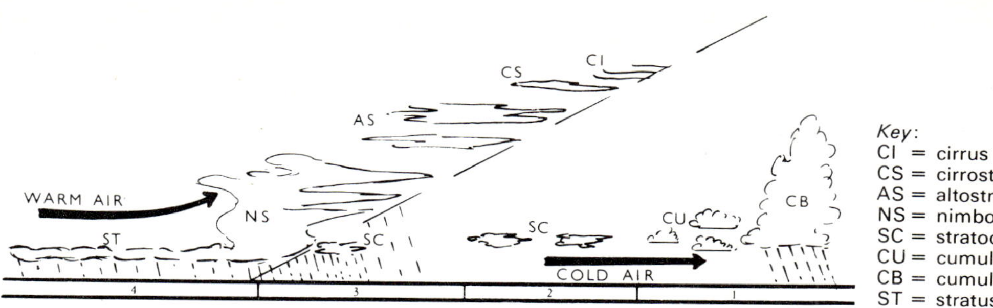

Key:
CI = cirrus
CS = cirrostratus
AS = altostratus
NS = nimbostratus
SC = stratocumulus
CU = cumulus
CB = cumulonimbus
ST = stratus

FIG. 117 The passage of a warm front showing the sequence of events:
1 – Any showers will die out and cumulus clouds develop less as cirrus appear, usually in the west. A brief fine spell ensues.
2 – Layer clouds progressively thicken and lower. A halo may appear around sun or moon for a time before sun or moon becomes obscured. Wind will back and freshen a little.
3 – Rain commences and soon becomes steady. Cloud lowers further, wind freshens, and both temperature and humidity start to rise.
4 – Steady rain ceases. Low cloud usually remains, often with drizzle. Temperature and humidity now remain steady. Wind veers and usually decreases.

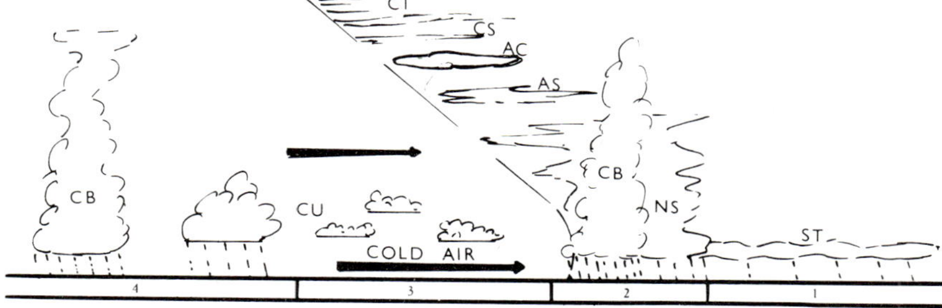

Key:
CI = cirrus
CS = cirrostratus
AC = altocumulus
AS = altostratus
NS = nimbostratus
ST = stratus
CB = cumulonimbus
CU = cumulus.

FIG. 118 The passage of a cold front showing the sequence of events:
1 – Warm sector conditions prevail with stratus and drizzle.
2 – Layer cloud thickens and drizzle becomes steady rain, sometimes the lifting of the warm air by the cold produces a cumulonimbus cloud and a burst of heavy rain, maybe with thunder, occurs on the front.
3 – Usually a little way behind the cold front a fairly sharp clearance occurs and the sun appears. Small cumulus will be developing upwind. The air is cooler and fresher and the wind will have veered.
4 – Cumulus clouds increase in size if the cold air is deep, and showers occur eventually if a ridge is following the cold front; shower activity may be only brief.

an hour or so the clearance should have arrived. There is often a brief fine spell behind the cold front before showers develop as the cold air 'deepens' and cumulonimbus clouds form. With a weak cold front there may be little or no shower activity behind it, whilst in a very unsettled situation the showers may be frequent and commence as soon as the front is through. Another feature of the passage of a cold front is that visibility often improves greatly because the front usually introduces unpolluted clear air from polar regions.

The occluded front acts like a warm front ahead of it and a cold front behind it, with no 'warm sector' in between. With a steadily moving occlusion the whole sequence may pass by in several hours but, in winter and spring, these fronts may get slowed down over western Britain by anti-cyclones over Scandinavia and they can then give persistent snowfall in the hills, with the cold polar continental air ahead of them.

From careful visual observation it is therefore possible to locate your approximate position in relation to a system and to estimate what further changes may or may not take place.

Weather Lore

Weather sayings have been used for hundreds of years. However, traditional forecasting cannot in any way compare with the scientific approach of the modern weatherman. The main limitation of traditional forecasting is that the observer can only make his prediction from visual data comparatively close to him whereas the meteorologist has an overall weather picture of a large land mass. Nevertheless, in isolated country there are times when it is not possible to obtain a weather forecast, perhaps due to faulty or difficult radio reception or a lack of telephone facilities to meteorological centres. At this stage you are completely dependent on your own local observations. Some of the traditional indications on which man has based his forecasts for the weather are listed below. It cannot be claimed that any individual indication can be in any way conclusive. The weather observer therefore needs to note the presence of several natural indications before coming to a conclusion:

(a) *Fair Weather*
White moon
Red sunset
Morning fog
Overnight heavy dew
Smoke rises vertically
Skies are cloudless
Drifting cumulus or stationary cirrus clouds
Rainbow in the evening

(b) *Bad Weather*
Ring around the moon (particularly in summer)

Halo around the sun (particularly in summer)
Very clear visibility
High wispy cirrus clouds building up from the south-west
Stratus and nimbus clouds
Dark clouds on the horizon
Clouds moving in various directions at different heights
Strengthening of the wind
Wind backing from west to south or south-east (in northern hemisphere)
No overnight dew
Crickets and other sounds seem very loud due to the atmospheric conditions
Red sky in the morning
Dull sunset
Yellow or orange moon when overhead
Rainbow in the morning
Muggy, sticky atmosphere
Smoke rises a short distance, then drifts to low places

Developing Forecast Technique

Technique and knowledge of weather forecasting can be developed by taking a regular close interest in television forecasts and weather maps, radio forecasts and also the forecasts given in newspapers, particularly those papers that give a forecast map in addition to a report map. After reading or listening to daily forecasts, carefully observe the weather so that you can, for example, identify the characteristics on land, say, of a moderate gale of Force 7, or of the type of cloud spreading from the south-west, etc. Learn the cloud sequence that heralds the arrival of a cold or a warm front; also learn the expressions that can signify bad mountain weather approaching such as: depression, front, increase in cloud, increase in wind, falling pressure, low pressure. Take note and memorize the words that signify good mountain weather approaching: high pressure, anti-cyclone, rising pressure, light winds or calm, frost and fog warnings, clear skies. Your practice should progress to interpreting data on weather maps without reference to the text then checking your interpretation with the official forecast. Progress further to making a visual weather forecast and then check your predictions against the official forecast.

Weather forecasting in the mountains is a skill that is based on experience, continual observation of local conditions and the ability to interpret the weather's features. However, always bear in mind that the 'met-man' can give the most accurate predictions as to the weather so, if you have access to a telephone weather-service or can telephone the 'met-man' at a local flying station or weather centre, use these facilities. Also listen to the national and local weather forecast on the radio. It is, in the interests of safety, imperative that the leader of a mountain walk knows what weather conditions to expect in the hills.

APPENDIX A

The Country Code

All users of the hills and mountains should observe the Country Code:

1. Guard against all risks of fire.
2. Fasten all gates.
3. Keep dogs under proper control.
4. Keep to paths across farmland.
5. Avoid damaging fences, hedges and walls.
6. Do not leave litter.
7. Safeguard water supplies.
8. Protect wildlife, wild plants and trees.
9. Go carefully on country roads.
10. Respect the life of the countryside.

APPENDIX B

Summary of the Mountain Leader Training Scheme (Summer)

The Mountain Leader Training Scheme (Summer) of the United Kingdom Mountain Leader Training Boards covers the skills and techniques required to take a party on walking and camping expeditions in mountainous areas of the United Kingdom under normal summer conditions. The scheme has particular merit for youth leaders, teachers and other adults involved in the preparation of young people for mountain walking projects and the actual leadership of parties. The scheme incorporates basic training followed by mandatory practical experience after which candidates are assessed.

Basic Training

Basic training is carried out over a period of at least a week or four weekends at a centre approved by the Mountain Leader Training Board. Candidates for basic training must be at least eighteen years. The course covers the following subjects:

1. Map and compass
2. Route planning
3. Walking skills
4. Personal equipment
5. Camping equipment
6. Campcraft
7. Security on steep ground
8. River crossing
9. Special mountain hazards
10. Weather
11. Accident procedure
12. Information on clubs and guide books
13. Responsibilities of party leader
14. Related interests

Practical Experience

Practical experience in mountaincraft of at least one year gained during weekends and holidays is to be obtained. During this period the candidates must:

(a) Obtain a current adult certificate in first aid, as issued by the British Red Cross Society, the St John Ambulance Association, or the Armed Services First Aid Certificate. The certificate must be obtained prior to assessment.

(b) Keep a log book record of every expedition accomplished within the period. These expeditions should include not less than sixteen days spent in mountainous country and at least half of this time should involve camping. It is suggested as a guide that candidates should have climbed about thirty named peaks of 2,000-3,000 ft (600-1000 m) in more than one mountain area.

(c) Thoroughly practise the skills learned at basic training, i.e. map and compass work, campcraft, etc. Further practice in rock climbing should only be taken under expert guidance.

(d) Obtain practice in leading and instructing small parties of novices in easy hill country.

Assessment

Candidates are required to attend a final residential week of assessment at a centre approved by the Board. During this period candidates will be tested as to their technical ability and leadership in accordance with the requirements of the Mountain Leader Training Scheme (Summer) syllabus. Candidates must be at least twenty years old before they can obtain a recommendation from the Mountain Leader Training Board.

Full details of the Mountain Leader Training Scheme (Summer) can be obtained from the Mountain Leader Training Board, Crawford House, Precinct Centre, Booth Street East, Manchester, M13 9RZ.

APPENDIX C

Clothing and Equipment - Summer Projects

The following list of clothing and equipment is given as a guide though some variation may be necessary according to the type of terrain and weather conditions anticipated:

LOW-LEVEL ONE-DAY WALK

Clothing
Anorak
Sweater
Boots
Stockings (plus reserve)
Trousers/breeches
Shirt
Cap *
Over-trousers *
Gaiters *

HIGH-LEVEL ONE-DAY WALK

Clothing
Cagoule
Anorak
Boots
Stockings (plus reserve)
Trousers/breeches
Shirt
2 sweaters
Gloves *
Cap *
Over-trousers *
Gaiters *

* *according to conditions*

LOW-LEVEL ONE-DAY WALK

Equipment
Rucksack (1:3)
Cagoule or polythene survival bag (6 x 3 ft)
Map
Compass
Watch
Whistle
Torch (1:3)
First-aid kit
Pocket knife
Matches
Pencil
Water bottle
Sunglasses
Suncream

Food
Day rations
Emergency rations

Leader's Additional Equipment
First-aid kit

HIGH-LEVEL ONE-DAY WALK

Equipment
Rucksack
Polythene survival bag (6 x 3 ft)
Map
Compass
Watch
Whistle
Torch (1:3)
First-aid kit
Pocket knife
Matches
Pencil
Water bottle
Sunglasses
Suncream

Food
Day rations
Emergency rations

Leader's Additional Equipment
First-aid kit
120 ft (36 m), 9 mm (3/8 in.) nylon rope
Red flares
Sleeping bag

LOW-LEVEL EXPEDITION

Clothing
Clothing as noted above for low-level one-day walk plus extra shirts, socks, underclothes, pair of trousers and light plimsolls

HIGH-LEVEL EXPEDITION

Clothing
Clothing as noted above for high-level one-day walk plus extra shirts, socks, underclothes, pair of trousers and light plimsolls

LOW-LEVEL EXPEDITION

Equipment

Equipment as noted above for low-level one-day walk but with one rucksack per person plus:

Tent (1:2)
Sleeping bag
Hip-length air-bed or foam mat
Stove (1:3)
Fuel
Cooking utensils (1:3)
Eating utensils
Knife, fork and spoon
Mug
Tin opener (1:3)
Trowel (1:6)
Toilet kit
Small towel
String
Candles (to save batteries)
Brillo pads
Water-purifying tablets
Torch
Boot polish (1:6)
Repair kit (for clothes and tent) (1:6)

Food

Rations for period plus emergency rations

Leader's Additional Equipment

First-aid kit
120 ft (36 m), 9 mm ($\frac{3}{8}$ in.) nylon rope
Small good transistor radio (for weather forecasts)
Spare battery

HIGH-LEVEL EXPEDITION

Equipment

Equipment as noted above for high-level one-day walk plus:

Mountain-type tent
Sleeping bag (cold-weather type)
Hip-length air-bed or foam mat
Stove (1:3)
Fuel
Cooking utensils (1:3)
Eating utensils
Knife, fork and spoon
Mug
Tin opener (1:3)
Trowel (1:6)
Toilet kit
Small towel
String
Candles (to save batteries)
Brillo pads
Water-purifying tablets
Torch
Boot polish (1:6)
Repair kit (for clothes and tent) (1:6)

Food

Rations for period plus emergency rations

Leader's Additional Equipment

First-aid kit
120 ft (36 mm), 9 mm ($\frac{3}{8}$ in.) nylon rope
Red flares
Small good transistor radio (for weather forecasts)
Spare battery

APPENDIX D

Long-distance Footpaths of Britain

KEY
A Pennine Way (250 miles)
B Cleveland Way (93 miles)
C Offa's Dyke Path (168 miles)
D Pembrokeshire Coast Path (167 miles)
E North Downs Way (141 miles)
F South Downs Way (80 miles)
G Ridgeway Path (85 miles)
H South West Peninsula Coast Path (515 miles)

Index